THE TREES, SHRUBS, AND PLANTS
OF VIRGIL

THE TREES, SHRUBS, AND PLANTS OF VIRGIL

BY

JOHN SARGEAUNT

Select Bibliographies Reprint Series

BOOKS FOR LIBRARIES PRESS
FREEPORT, NEW YORK

First Published 1920
Reprinted 1969

STANDARD BOOK NUMBER:
8369-5098-4

LIBRARY OF CONGRESS CATALOG CARD NUMBER:
79-99669

PRINTED IN THE UNITED STATES OF AMERICA

PREFACE

IN the sixteenth century several botanists interested themselves in the plants of the ancient Romans. Among them were two able Italians, Pietro Andrea Mathioli (1500-1577), whose name has been given to the cruciferous genus of stock, and Andrea Cesalpini (1519-1603), from whom is named the leguminous genus of Caesalpinia. Over Dodoens or Dodonaeus they had the advantage of being natives and inhabitants of Italy. Their works were studied by John Martyn, Professor of Botany in the University of Cambridge, who in 1741 published an edition of the Georgics with an English translation. His works deal with the substance rather than with the language of Virgil's poem. He had been for some years in correspondence with Linné, from whom he probably received help. Although Linné was occasionally in error, a list of the scientific names will show how skilfully he had studied the ancient Roman writings. Martyn made two or three bad blunders, but his book is a monument of clear observation and sound common sense. It was followed in 1749 by an edition of the Eclogues. At

Preface

later dates several French botanists published Floras of Virgil. In view of more recent discoveries their conclusions cannot always be accepted, and, as their works have long been out of print, there seems room for the present little work.

The *Flora Italiana* of Dr. Giovanni Arcangeli (2nd edition, Turin, 1896) is useful in its records of the present geographical range of Virgil's plants. Of later knowledge, perhaps the most notable discovery is the difference between the Italian and the English elms, but Arcangeli was able to accept incidentally Boissier's identification of Virgil's *phaselus* with the plant known in Italy as *fagiolo dall' occhio*. Although Virgil directs the sowing of it in autumn, even Martyn, followed by many editors, identified it with the tender French bean, which probably did not find its way to Europe before the days of Queen Elizabeth.

It is to be regretted that Conington, who gave much thought to Virgil, had little interest in natural objects. His notes on plants are sometimes grotesquely in error. It is, however, to another child of the cloister that readers of the ancient pastoral poems owe the information that birds follow the plough in order to pick up the grain. Unless a benevolent ploughman sowed it with his heels, the birds must have made a poor living of it. Birds do pick up grain, but not behind the plough. Perhaps the obituary of the house of Grub could provide a more mournful explanation.

I ought to say that with two or three plants on my

Preface

list I am acquainted only through descriptions and figures. On the other hand, I have nearly half of them growing in my garden, and others are to be found near at hand.

The addition of plants from *Moretum* and *Copa* will, I hope, be welcome, and not be taken as necessarily involving any view on the authenticity of those poems.

FAIRWARP,
SUSSEX,
1919.

THE TREES, SHRUBS, AND PLANTS OF VIRGIL

INTRODUCTION

By descent and birth Virgil was not an Italian but a Gaul, and at the time of his birth his father was not a Roman citizen. Nevertheless, Latin civilization was already entirely at home in the plain of the Po, and had brought with it the Hellenic strain which runs through the whole of the Eclogues. Thus Virgil was not afraid to call Italy his own country, even without reference to the share of Tuscan blood which he believed to be possessed by the men of Mantova. Thus, when he came in the second Georgic to celebrate the praises of Italy, it hardly needed the extension of the franchise to justify him in ignoring the boundary made by the Apennines and the little brook of Rubicon. In his encomium of Italian valour the Ligurian takes his place beside the Marsian and the Samnite, and the lakes of Como and Garda are no less Italian than the Tyrrhene surge which sweeps into the haven of Avernus.

In the youthful Virgil there were two characteristics which were not always at one. He had a native love of observation and he had a young man's passion for the beautiful language of the Greek pastoral poets.

His power of observation may well have been inherited, and we can hardly doubt that it was encouraged by the parents who made a push to give him a gentleman's education. It was not driven out of him by the training in bad rhetoric which poisoned for him the last days of his school life. He saw natural objects with a clearness which in later days sometimes deserted him when he came to describe the scenes and incidents of an epic poem. We do well to call the Aeneid his greatest work, but its greatness is other than that of the Georgics.

Martyn calls attention to the exactness with which his poet characterizes a group of willows, 'glauca canentia fronde salicta.' 'The leaves,' as he says, 'are of a bluish green, and the under side of them is covered with white down.' This is not true of all willows, but is true of the species which Virgil had in mind. For a more detailed description and an attempt to create an exact vocabulary reference may be made to the article on 'Amellus.' For an attempt to give on the authority of authors a clear account of a tree of which he can have seen only the fruit we may refer to the article on the citron.

Beside this power of observation, there is in Virgil's earliest work the literary strain which is not always in accord with it. Wordsworth has told us that English poetry published between the years 1668

2

Introduction

and 1726 does not, with two exceptions, 'contain
a single new image of external nature.' One of the
exceptions is 'a passage or two' in the earlier work
of Pope. Although Pope and Virgil were destined
to develop on very different lines, there was a touch
of likeness in their earlier works, and Pope's juvenilia
stand somewhat to Virgil's pastorals as Virgil's stand
to the works of Theocritus and Moschus. Virgil
seems at times to think less of the objects with
which he deals than of his desire to reproduce in
the graver, not to say heavier, language of Rome
the beauties of the Sicilian poets. My subject does
not call for any defence of the Eclogues. It might
else be necessary to contend that the pastoral form
of these poems is not to be accused of affectation
or falsehood. It is the vehicle by which a young
poet expresses his view of beauty and of the purpose
and passions of life.

Now when Theocritus tells us that the goat goes
in quest of cytisus and the wolf in quest of the
goat, we may well believe that he had seen the goat
browsing on the shrub and the wolf coming down
from the hills. But the shrub did not come within
many miles of Mantova, and, although the possi-
bility of Alpine wolves occasionally descending upon
the plain cannot be denied, we cannot be certain
that Virgil had yet seen one. If Virgil, when he
wrote the fourth Eclogue, had ever seen a tamarisk,
he would probably have chosen some other epithet
than *humilis* to represent the shrub as the emblem
of lowly poetry; for the word might suggest that the

3

Trees, Shrubs, and Plants of Virgil

shrub itself is never tall, whereas sometimes it is almost a tree.

It must be admitted that even in his more mature work Virgil sometimes accepted statements from others, and took no pains to see that they were true. Thus he had heard that any scion could be successfully grafted on any stock. On the strength of this information he fancied pear blossoms covering with white the branches of the manna ash, and swept away by his poetic fervour conceived of swine champing acorns under an elm. Columella tried to save his master's credit in this matter by showing how such grafting could succeed. It is, however, manifest that in Columella's subterranean grafting the scion makes roots not in the stock, but in the ground, and is, in fact, not a grafted scion, but a cutting.

The names of colours present great difficulties. The colour sense, especially in reds and blues, seems to have developed rather late in man's history. The yellows are fairly clear, except that there seems to be no word which clearly indicates the shining yellow of the buttercup. Both *croceus*, which comes from the stigmata of the saffron crocus, and *luteus* or *luteolus*, which come from the dye of weld, seem to have a dash of orange in them. Virgil in one place combines them and speaks of saffron weld. The yolk of an egg was always called *luteum*. Then comes *flavus*, which is used most of fields of ripe corn, but also of the yellow sands, an auburn head of hair, and gold. Gold is also called *fulvum*, much as we speak of red gold; for of this hue is the tawny hide of the

4

Introduction

lion, and even the less red hide of the wolf. Last is *gilvus*, which is dun, and is used of a horse.

Then there are white and black. It seems clear that Virgil does not distinguish *candidus* and *albus*, for he applies them both to the same objects. The original meaning of *candidus* was white hot, and it therefore implies a shining white, but Virgil applies it to a beard and a poplar-tree. Nor can it be made out that he distinguishes *ater* and *niger* except in metaphorical uses. Properly *ater* seems to be the colour of charcoal. There is also a wide extension both of black and of white. Of two Sicilians one is called black and the other white. A black flower need be no darker than violet, and we may say that in some contexts white means little more than not black and black little more than not white.

Worst of all are the two words *purpureus* and *ferrugineus*. As applied to flowers, the former appears to mean no more than bright, a meaning which it retains when applied to the light of youth— 'lumen iuventae.' A contemporary of Virgil applied the epithet to snow, and I cannot see that Virgil ever uses it of a dark hue, not even when he applies it to the breath or soul leaving the body in a violent death. On the other hand, *ferrugineus*, which must originally have signified the colour of iron rust, does connote some darkness, and clearly Virgil uses it of Tyrian purple. He also uses it of the darkness that comes over the sun in an eclipse and of Charon's boat. A character in Plautus tells us that it is the colour of the sea, and as the sea displays so many colours he was doubtless in part right. It seems, however, that none of these uses would make it impossible for a Roman to apply the word to some shade of red. On the *hyacinthus* we cannot rule reds out on the ground that Virgil writes of 'ferrugineos hyacinthos.'

Another difficulty is that we are not always sure whether Virgil's epithet applies to the whole of a blossom or part of it, whether to the blossom at all or to the leaves or some other part. Sometimes we can see him using an epithet as we should not. Thus to a Latin the important part of a poppy is the seeds, and, because the seeds are small, Virgil writes of the small poppy, though the plant will out-top a man. Again, as we see in Theophrastus, when the stamens and pistils of a flower were large they were regarded as a second flower within the other. The Greek writes thus, for instance, of the lily and the rose. Thus when Virgil writes 'purpureo narcisso' he seems to me to refer to the shining white of the outer perianth; but to some he seems to speak of the cup, which Arcangeli calls scarlet, and Nicholson, perhaps more correctly, scarlet-edged. There can be no doubt that in 'pallentes hederae' the epithet applies solely to the fruit.

From the writers on country affairs, especially Pliny and Columella, some help is obtained on these points. They also aid us to ascertain things which were probably known to Virgil, though they are not mentioned in his works.

6

Introduction

It is, perhaps, not superfluous to say that the lexicons err at times, not only in their identification of the plants, but also in the names of their parts. Several examples will be found in the text. One may be mentioned here. The lexicons say that both *palmes* and *pampinus* mean a vine-tendril. In fact, they have different meanings, but the meaning of tendril belongs to neither.

It may be well to set forth the various meanings of some of the Latin words used of plants, as the lexicons are defective in this matter.

Folium usually means a leaf, but it also is used to signify the petals of a polypetalous flower, such as the poppy; the ray-flowers of a composite, such as the daisy; and the divisions of the perianth in monocotyledons, such as the lily. Further, it may mean a spray or branchlet of any coniferous tree, or the tunics of the bulb in such plants as squills.

Ramus normally means a branch or bough, but Virgil also uses it of the male catkins of the walnut.

Filum, from its sense of a thread, comes to mean the filament of a stamen. Since, by a metaphor from weaving, it sometimes signifies the outline or contour of a human or other figure, it is used for the habit of a plant, and, it would seem, also for its stem.

Silva may signify the flowering stems of any plant that has more than one, such as lupins and Michaelmas daisies.

Cespes, which properly means a sod, may be used of a stool—that is to say, a mass of roots in a plant which makes offshoots, as the Michaelmas daisy.

THE TREES, SHRUBS, AND PLANTS
OF VIRGIL

ABIES.

'casus abies visura marinos' (*Ge.* ii. 68).
'pulcherrima . . . abies in montibus altis' (*Ec.* vii. 66).
'nigra . . . abiete' (*Ae.* viii. 599).

The red or silver fir (Abies pectinata) is common on the Alps, and occurs, though seldom in great quantity, through the range of the Apennines, where Theophrastus notes that it grew to a great size. Byron knew it, though not as Virgil's tree; and in the lines,

'But from their nature will the tannen grow
Loftiest on loftiest and least shelter'd rocks'

(*C.H.P.* iv. 20),

he naturalized its German name, a fact overlooked by the *N.E.D.* In a note he adds that it is the tallest mountain tree, a statement true of Europe. It runs up to a hundred feet. The timber was used in shipbuilding, and on account of its lightness preferred to all others for masts and yard-arms.

Since a large mass of this fir as seen in the distance looks black, especially against the sky, Virgil's epithet is justified. The Romans, however, generally called evergreen trees black in contrast with the usually lighter foliage of deciduous species.

Flower, March to May.
Italian name, Abete rosso.

Acanthus

A. ' molli circum est ansas amplexus acantho' (*Ec.* iii. 45).
B. ' circumtextum croceo velamen acantho' (*Ae.* i. 649).
' baccas semper frondentis acanthi' (*Ge.* ii. 119).

Here we have two distinct plants under one name.
The former is our garden bear's-breech (Acanthus
mollis), a scrofularious plant with a dull flower and
the large leaves which were long thought to have
suggested the Corinthian capital. In Theocritus the
carving is in relief on the body of the cup; Virgil
transfers it to the handles, and perhaps meant it to
represent the flower spike. The epithet of 'mollis'
both alludes to the carver's skill, and distinguishes
the plant from a kindred species whose leaves end in
short spines.

Flower, March to July.
Italian names, Acanto and Brancorsina.

The other plant is gum arabic (Acacia Arabica),
which is not native in Italy, and with us is a greenhouse tree. It is akin to the shrubs whose sprays
of yellow flowers are in spring imported from the
Riviera to London, and sold under the name of
mimosa. These are of Australian origin. The
flowers of our plant are in globular heads. By
'baccas' Virgil means either these heads or the
curious seed-pod, which resembles a string of beads.

In *Ge.* iv. 123 is the difficult phrase 'flexi vimen
acanthi,' referred by Martyn to the bear's-breech,
though neither the substantive nor the adjective well
fits this plant. He finds an explanation in a story

9

Trees, Shrubs, and Plants of Virgil

told by Vitruvius, who says that a basket covered with a tile happened to be placed upon a root of acanthus, and when the plant shot up in spring the stalks came up round the basket till they were caused by the tile to bend outward. The architect Callimachus, passing by, was struck by the effect, and, having to make some pillars at Corinth, imitated it in the capitals. The story, probably a fiction, may have been known to Virgil, but is not satisfactory as an explanation of our passage. It is better to refer Virgil's phrase to the gum arabic, and to suppose that in favourable spots in Italy, such as the Corycian's garden at Taranto, the plant could be grown in the open air with such protection in winter as in the north was given to myrtles. With us it is a greenhouse tree.

The robe which Leda made for Helen had a woven border representing our plant.

> Flower, spring.
> Italian name, Acacia.

ACER.

> 'trabibus . . . acernis' (*Ae.* ii. 112 ; ix. 87).
> 'solio . . . acerno' (*Ae.* viii. 178).

The maple (Acer campestre), both in Greece and in Italy mainly a tree of the hills, disappears in southern Italy, but is found again on the mountains of Sicily. Virgil gives it, together with pine and spruce, as supplying the timber for the wooden horse, and he doubtless thought of them as trees of Mount Ida. In our second passage 'trabibus' is used

Aconitum

of living trees, which form part of a sacred grove of
Cybele. The maple throne of Evander marks the
simplicity of the Arcadian exile's life. Silver and
gold he had none.

Maple wood is hard, and was used for the yokes of
oxen and for writing tablets. It was a favourite
material with the wealthy for tables, either entire or
veneered; and Pliny says it was second only to what
the Romans called citron—that is, the wood of
Juniperus oxycedrus.

Flower, April and May.
Italian names, Acero, Chioppo, and Loppo.

ACONITUM.
    ' nec miseros fallunt aconita legentes ' (*Ge.* ii. 152).
    'fallax herba veneni' (*Ec.* iv. 24).

Dioscorides has distressed the commentators by
saying that there were aconites in Italy, but the
species to which he refers were probably well known
as poisonous. Virgil is speaking of a noxious plant
which was liable to be confounded with a harmless
one, and probably means the pale yellow monk's-
hood (Aconitum anthora), a near relative of our
own blue and poisonous monk's-hood, which is sometimes mistaken for horseradish. Virgil might justly
say that his country was exempt from the danger of
this plant, for its only claim to a place in the Italian
flora is that it occurs in the mountains of Liguria.
There is nothing to show that Virgil had ever seen
the plant, but he had read of it in the Greek authors,

Trees, Shrubs, and Plants of Virgil

and learnt from them that there was no known antidote.

Flower, July and August.

AESCULUS: see Robur.

ALGA.

'saxa frenunt laterique illisa refunditur alga' (*Ae.* vii. 590).
'proiecta vilior alga' (*Ec.* vii. 42).

This was a general name for various kinds of sea-weed. They are not entirely worthless, for one yields a red dye, and Palladius was aware of their value as manure. Columella also recommends its use in transplanting cabbage. Dulse appears to have been unknown. Since much of the seaweed cast up on the shore was wasted, and that which was used cost no more than the labour of moving it, seaweed came to be a synonym for what is worthless.

ALIUM.

'alia serpyllumque herbas contundit olentes' (*Ec.* ii. 11).

That Virgil is justified in the epithet which he assigns to garlic (Allium sativum) no one who has sat beside an Italian or Sicilian driver will care to dispute. The plant is Asiatic, but early found its way into Greece and Italy, and in both countries it was regarded as giving both courage and strength to him that ate it. In our passage the leaves are bruised together with thyme for the reapers' midday meal. This salad included flour and cheese with oil

Alnus

and vinegar. Its name was 'moretum,' and the poem with that title, ascribed to Virgil, supplies this work with some names of plants.

> Flower, June and July.
> Italian name, Aglio.

ALNUS.

> 'crassis . . . paludibus alni | nascuntur' (*Ge.* ii. 110).
> 'tunc alnos primum fluvii sensere cavatas' (*Ge.* i. 136).

The alder (Alnus glutinosa) is a common tree along river-banks in most parts of Europe, and goes up to three thousand feet above sea-level on the Apennines. It is akin to the birch, which in Italy is confined to sub-alpine districts and is not mentioned by Virgil. The hollowed trunk supplied an early, though perhaps not the earliest, form of a boat. It is plentiful on the Po, where it seems still to have been used for boat-building in Virgil's days: 'innatat alnus missa Pado' (*Ge.* ii. 451). The flowers and fruits are in a somewhat inelegant catkin, which appears before the leaves. Hence the jilted shepherd, in praying for an inversion of Nature, desires that the blossoms of the poet's narcissus may appear upon the alder: 'narcisso floreat alnus' (*Ec.* viii. 53). Virgil notices the very rapid growth of alder shoots. in spring (*Ec.* x. 74).

> Flower, March.
> Italian name, Ontano.

13

Trees, Shrubs, and Plants of Virgil

Amaracus.

'mollis amaracus illum | floribus et dulci adspirans complectitur umbra' (*Ae.* i. 693).

The sweet marjoram (Origanum majorana) is a North African herb, which has been in our gardens since the days of Elizabeth. As it will not stand our winters, it is treated here as an annual. It is naturalized in Italy, and Virgil may have known it as a garden plant. Since, however, the passage deals with a miracle of Venus, we need not assume this. The plant was used for wreaths.

Our plant seems to be Shakespeare's sweet marjoram, though our old writers ascribe sweetness and other virtues to the native species also. They belong to the labiate order, and are akin to thyme and mint.

> Flower, June and July.
> Italian names, Maggiorana and Persia.

Amellus.

> 'est etiam flos in pratis cui nomen amello
> fecere agricolae, facilis quaerentibus herba ;
> namque uno ingentem tollit de cespite silvam ;
> aureus ipse, sed in foliis, quae plurima circum
> funduntur, violae sublucet purpura nigrae.
> saepe deum nexis ornatae torquibus arae.
> asper in ore sapor : tonsis in vallibus illum
> pastores et curva legunt prope flumina Mellae.'
> (*Ge.* iv. 271 sqq.)

Here we have Virgil describing solely from his own observation a plant of his own district with what we may presume to be a Gallic name. It does

Amellus

not extend into southern Italy, and it is clear that
Columella never saw it, and mistook Virgil's description of it.   There seems to be no certain mention of
it in any other ancient author.

The plant is the Aster amellus of Linnaeus, one of
the many species to which our gardeners have given
the name of Michaelmas daisies.   Virgil had no
technical vocabulary for botanical descriptions, but
in this case he almost creates one.   The flower is a
composite, the head consisting of disk flowers and
ray flowers.   His name for the disk is *flos ipse*, and
his name for the ray flowers is *folia*, a word which
Ovid applies to the petaloid perianth of a lily, just
as φύλλον is one name for a petal.   What gardeners
call the stool—that is, the mass of roots and sub-
terranean stems—is ' cespes,' and the stems which
rise from it are the ' ingens silva.'   When Virgil
says that in the ray flowers purple shines under dark
violet, he seems to indicate a particular shade of
purple or violet for which there was no name.   Our
earlier translators made sad work of a passage which
is as clear as Virgil's vocabulary could make it.

The Mella is a tributary of the Po, which rises
in the mountains above Brescia, and Virgil here
refers to its upper course, for the plant does not
descend into the plains.   It grows on the sides of the
valleys, and is conspicuous in August and September,
when the grass has been shortened by mowing or
grazing.   We may take ' tonsis ' in either sense, for
the effect is the same.   The latter sense seems more
likely, for, although the plant is not full grown at

the time of the hay harvest, it is tall enough to be topped by the scythe. Moreover, it affects the slopes rather than the level ground.

Under cultivation and through hybridizing amellus has developed many varieties. In many of them the disk has taken the colour of the rays. Whether it ever does this in the wild state I do not know.

Virgil recommends boiling the roots in wine as a remedy for bee disease. The taste, as he says, is rough, and the Brescian bee-keepers may have known their business when they gave the root to the sick bees.

> Flower, July to October.
> Italian names, Amello and Astro.

AMOMUM.

> 'ferat et rubus asper amomum' (*Ec.* iii. 89).
> 'Assyrium . . . amomum' (*Ec.* iv. 25).

Virgil cannot have known this East Indian shrub, which is akin to the banana and the plantain, though he knew the balsam which it produced. It is cardamom (Amomum cardamomum), and the spice yielded by its seed capsules fetched a high price at Rome. It has been cultivated in our stoves for nearly a hundred years, but its brownish flowers are not very attractive.

> Flower, summer.
> Italian name, Cardamomo.

Anethum

ANETHUM.

> 'florem bene olentis anethi' (*Ec.* ii. 48).
> 'vetus adstricti fascis pendebat anethi' (*Mor.* 59).

In our first passage Virgil follows the Sicilian poets, and probably did not know what plant he meant. In Greek the name usually meant dill; but it may well be doubted whether in Sicily, where this plant was not native, the name was not applied to the nearest native species. This was fennel (Foeniculum vulgare), a common plant in the lower ground of Italy and Sicily. When it was gathered the bunches were dried in the sun and used in cookery.

In Pliny and other writers our name means 'dill' (Anethum graveolens). The dried leaves were used to flavour soups.

> Flower, July and August.
> Italian name, Finocchio (fennel).
> Aneto (dill).

APIUM.

> 'virides apio ripae' (*Ge.* iv. 121).
> 'apio crines ornatus amaro' (*Ec.* vi. 68).

The lexicons call this plant parsley, but they are certainly wrong, as Virgil's epithet alone should have shown them. His plant is smallage or celery (Apium graveolens), the Greek σέλινον, which gave its name to the Sicilian city. Celery likes to grow, where Virgil puts it, with its toes in water; while parsley, nowhere known as a wild plant, naturalizes itself, as Hooker says, ' on castle walls and in waste places.' In a wild state celery is rank, coarse, and unwholesome; but it has been much improved by cultivation, and the bitterness, to which Virgil refers, is annulled by blanching the leaf-stems. For this purpose we earth it up, but Columella and Palladius recommend the use of a 'cylindrus,' which in this context clearly means a sea-kale pot or something like it.

The leaves were used in garlands and chaplets. An Italian scholar has in his possession a wreath taken from the heart of a mummy made in the fifteenth century B.C. It is composed of alternating leaves of celery and buds of the blue water-lily of the Nile.

Theophrastus refers to what seem to be cultivated varieties, and regards the plant as an effective remedy for the stone.

Flower, June.

Italian name, Sedano.

ARBUTUS.

'arbutus horrida' (*Ge.* ii. 69).
'vos rara viridis tegit arbutus umbra' (*Ec.* vii. 46. Cf. *Ec.* iii. 82 ; *Ge.* i. 148 ; ii. 69, 520 ; iii. 301 ; iv. 181).

The arbute (Arbutus unedo) is a tree of the Mediterranean region, which extends northwards to Killarney. It is called the strawberry-tree from a superficial resemblance in the scarlet fruit, called by Lucretius 'puniceus'; but the tubercles on the surface are not, as in the strawberry, the seeds.

Arbutus

Pliny's name of 'unedo' was supposed to mean that he who ate one would never eat another, but Italian peasants do eat it when it is quite ripe. Both leaves and fruit seem to have been a favourite food of goats—'dulcis depulsis arbutus haedis' (*Ec.* iii. 82). Virgil makes bees feed on it (*Ge.* iv. 181), but the flowers come too late in the year to be of much use for honey. The bark of the stems is very rough, and to this Virgil's epithet alludes. Hurdles were made of the wood (*Ge.* i. 166).

In our gardens the tree will grow to the height of ten feet, and in autumn displays both flowers and ripe fruits.

> Flower, autumn.
> Italian names, Albatro and Corbezzolo.

AVENA AND AVENA STERILIS.

> 'urit enim campum lini seges, urit avenae' (*Ge.* i. 77).
> 'steriles nascuntur avenae' (*Ec.* v. 37).
> 'steriles dominantur avenae' (*Ge.* i. 154).

The two plants are of different species, but the Romans gave them one name, and held that the wild oat (Avena fatua) was a degeneracy from the cultivated oat (A. sativa), or from barley.

The oat is not a plant of southern climates, and in the central peninsula was probably cultivated only in Cisalpine Gaul, where Virgil, as a boy, must have seen it, and on the northern slopes of the Apennines. He was thus able to confirm the observation of Theophrastus that it 'runs' or exhausts the soil.

Trees, Shrubs, and Plants of Virgil

Columella says it should be cut green for fodder or hay. In comparing it to a wild plant the Greek authority does not mean that it was not cultivated, but refers to what he calls the many husks of the seed. The wild oat occurs all over Europe, and has increased in our cornfields since the beginning of the war. It is probable enough that the name of 'avena' was used of other grasses.

Although the straw of the oat can be made into a musical instrument, it is probable that our poets in dealing with it have not always had their eyes on the object. It was enough for them that Virgil used 'avena' of the pastoral instrument. Hence Spenser speaks of the shepherd who broke 'his oaten pipe,' Shakespeare of shepherds piping on 'oaten strawes,' and Milton of 'the oaten flute.' Of these three poets Milton was the most musical, and in this case the most inaccurate. A single straw could not be made into a flute, and even as a pipe could hardly make the woods resound in praise of Amaryllis. The fact is that 'avena' as a musical instrument is the pan-pipe, the accompanist in this country of the now, alas! obsolescent Punch and Judy show. This consisted of seven pipes, sometimes perhaps oaten straws, but more often reeds or kexes—'septem compacta cicutis fistula' (*Ec.* ii. 36). The single pipe was despised by a shepherd of musical powers, and left to those whose use it was 'stridenti miserum stipula disperdere caronen' (*Ec.* iii. 27), or to 'grate on their scrannel pipes of wretched straw.'

Within the memory of men living half a century

ago pan-pipes of straw were still made in remote parts of Oxfordshire, but even at that time the Punch and Judy men seem always to have employed reeds.

Italian name, Vena.

BACCAR.

> hederas passim cum baccare ' (*Ec.* iv. 19).
> ' baccare frontem cingite ' (*Ec.* vii. 27).

The name covers at least three species of cyclamen, only one of which, C. repandum, flowers in the spring. The other two species are autumnal, and geographically seem not to overlap, C. Europaeum not growing south of Lombardy and C. Neapolitanum not north of the Apennines. In Lombardy the former still bears the name of ' baccare,' but in the Apennines the only name I have ever got from the peasantry for either of the other species is ' scacciabile,' which doubtless refers to the purgative power. An allied species, C. hederaefolium, with a paler flower, is naturalized here and there in southern England. There is still considerable confusion in the nomenclature of these species.

The blossoms of the sowbreads, to give them their English name, are still made into nosegays and wreaths, not only in Italy, but also in the Tyrol, where children throw bunches of them into coaches and carriages and look for a reward. It is possible that there are districts where the flowers and the tubers are used, as they were in Theophrastus' time,

21

Trees, Shrubs, and Plants of Virgil

for love charms. The plants are hardy in this country and easy to cultivate in shade and leaf mould, to which it is well to add a little lime. They seed freely, but seedlings take some years to flower.

In our second passage Virgil treats the blossom as a prophylactic against curses and 'overlooking.' The Greeks used the powdered corm as a love charm.

The lexicons will have it that 'baccar' is the foxglove, though, as a native, that plant does not come nearer to Italy than Sardinia, and there seems to be no evidence that it was ever cultivated. Moreover, it is not well suited for a chaplet.

Visitors to Tivoli may find our plant on Monte Catillo above the railway station.

> Flower : C. Europaeum, June to October.
> C. repandum, April and May.
> C. Neapolitanum, September and October.
> Italian names : Pan-porcino, Pan-torreno, and Baccare.

BETA.

'late fundentes brachia betae' (*Mor.* 72).

The wild beet (Beta maritima) supplies nothing that is useful to man, but under cultivation it has developed what are called the roots of beet and of mangel-wurzel. Our passage shows that in Roman times the leaf also had increased in size, though probably not to the length of a yard or so, as in the modern variety known as Chilian beet. There were two kinds, of which the red must have been like our beet and the white like our mangel. As a vegetable neither was held in much account. What was most valued was the leaf of the species now called B. cicla. Columella describes this species as having green leaves and a white root.

Flower, July and August.

Italian name, Bietola.

BUXUS.

'undantem buxo spectare Cytorum' (*Ge.* ii. 437).

'torno rasile buxum' (*ib.* 449).

The box (Buxus sempervirens) is a rare native of Italy, as of England, but was largely grown in gardens, and suffered much from the topiary art. Virgil's line seems to imply a preference for it in its natural state, though he knew the woods of Cytorus, a mountain in Paphlagonia, only through his Greek authorities.

The slow-growing and hard wood is useful for various purposes. Virgil speaks of it as made into a frame for ivory (*Ae.* x. 136), and into a top (*Ae.* vii. 382); while the 'buxus Berecyntia matris Idaeae' (*Ae.* ix. 619) is a musical pipe. The cheapest form of writing tablets was made of boxwood and wax. Dennis mentions an Etruscan wreath of box sprays which was found in a tomb, but the Greek authorities do not seem to refer to box as a coronary tree.

It seems to have been the box and not, as Virgil

implies, the yew that gave the bitterness to Corsican honey.

> Flower, March and April.
> Italian names, Bosso and Bossolo.

CALAMUS.

The Greeks, from whom this word was borrowed, use it as a generic name for reeds, and distinguished many species, among which are our own common reed, Phraginites communis, sweet flag, Acorus calamus, and the fine grass, sometimes known as wood small-reed, Calamogrostis epigeios. Some of the Roman prose writers on country matters use the name generically of reeds and specifically of the sweet flag. In the poets it seems also to stand for the whole or part of the stem of a reed as put to some use, or, like the English halm, of the stem of some other plant, for instance, the lupin (*Ge.* i. 76). Virgil uses it once of reeds used as vine-props (*Ge.* ii. 358), once of an arrow (*Ae.* x. 140), and some eight times of a musical pipe. Virgil can hardly have failed to know the sweet flag, which grows on the Mincio as a native, and seems to have been imported for cultivation across the Apennines.

CALTHA, OR CALTA.

> ' mollia luteola pingit vaccinia caltha ' (*Ec.* ii. 50).

By a mistake Linnaeus gave this name to the marsh marigold, which, though a native of Italy,

Caltha, or Calta

cannot be Virgil's plant. Corydon's nosegay, of which it forms a part, could hardly be gathered at any one season, and gives us no guide to the flowering time of our plant. Not much is said of 'caltha' by our early authorities. For Virgil's epithet Columella substitutes flammeola, with a reference to the fiery orange tint of the bridal veil. From Pliny we learn that our plant had a strong scent, both in the leaves and in the blossom. All this points to the common pot marigold (Calendula officinalis), an African, brought early into cultivation for its use in condiments. The yellow ray flowers are still used in soups, and the plant has naturalized itself here and there both in Italy and in England.

Flower, July and August.

Italian names, Calendula and Fiorrancio.

CARDUUS.

'segnisque horreret in arvis | Carduus'

(*Ge.* i. 151 ; cf. *Ec.* v. 39).

Thistles are reckoned by Virgil among the plagues sent by the gods into the cultivated fields in order that the farmer might not have too easy a life. It is probable that several species are covered by the name, but in Italy, as with us, the worst enemy is the common field thistle (Carduus arvensis). It increases rapidly by means of stolons, and is hard to eradicate, because any broken bit of them will produce roots and stems. It is well that the flowers are often barren. Thus we may put aside Dr. Wood-

25

Trees, Shrubs, and Plants of Virgil

ward's calculation that a thistle three years old might have five hundred and seventy-six million grandchildren.

Another candidate is Centaurea solstitialis, St. Barnaby's thistle, a yellow-flowered annual very common in Italian cornfields. It is occasionally found in England, where the seeds have been introduced with those of lucerne. This, however, seems to be 'Tribulus,' q.v.

Pliny and other later writers give the name of 'carduus' to the esculent cardoon (Cynara cardunculus).

> Flower, summer.
> Italian names: Astone (Carduus).
> Spino giallo (Centaurea).

CAREX.

> 'carice pastus acuta' (*Ge.* iii. 231).
> 'tu post carecta latebas' (*Ec.* iii. 20).

Possibly several of the larger sedges are included in this name, but the best claim to be Virgil's plant is owned by that which still bears the names of 'carice' and 'caretta.' This is Carex acuta, which is common in Italy and its islands. The flowering stems are some three feet long, and the leaves equal them. It is rather common on the Thames and other English rivers, and, as Virgil implies, no satisfactory food for cattle.

> Flower, April and May.
> Italian names, Carice, Caretto, and Nocca.

Casia

CASIA.

A. 'humiles casias' (*Ge.* ii. 213).
   'casiae virides' (*Ge.* iv. 30 ; cf. *Ec.* ii. 49).
B. 'nec casia liquidi corrumpitur usus olivi' (*Ge.* ii. 466).

The two plants are quite distinct. The first is
a spurge-laurel (Daphne Gnidium), akin to the
spurge-laurel and the mezereon of our gardens. It
is a native of Italy, but seems not to occur on the
eastern side of the Apennines. It has a white flower,
which Virgil commends to bee-keepers, and a small
red berry, very acrid, but used in aperient pills under
the name of 'granum Gnidium.' The flowers were
used in garlands.

The second plant is the cinnamon of the Bible
(Laurus cinnamomum). It is an Oriental plant, and
was not cultivated in Italy, but the aromatic bark
was imported. It was used as a scent by men who
liked scent, with oil when used as an unguent, and
together with myrrh in funeral pyres.

Flower of Daphne, July to September.
Italian names of Daphne, Dittinella and
   Erbacorsa.

CASTANEA.

'altae castaneae' (*Ge.* ii. 14).
'castaneas molles' (*Ec.* i. 82).
'castaneae hirsutae' (*Ec.* vii. 53).
'castaneas . . . nuces' (*Ec.* ii. 52).

The sweet chestnut (Castanea sativa) is a tree of
uncertain provenance, for the fruit of which the

Trees, Shrubs, and Plants of Virgil

Latins had no single name. Pliny says, with some
reason, that it should rather be classed with the
glandes than with the nuces. The epithet of 'hirsutae'
refers to the prickly covering and 'molles' to the
roasted kernel, which was a common article of food.
Pliny thought little of it, and was surprised that
Nature had taken so much pains to protect so poor
a fruit. The best variety was known as Corellia,
and was supposed to have originated from a graft,
in which both stock and scion were of the same tree.
Chestnut bread was especially eaten by women at
fasting seasons.

In autumn the large leaves completely cover the
ground under the trees, whence comes Milton's
comparison:

> 'Thick as autumnal leaves that strew the brooks
> In Vallombrosa.'

The chestnut was largely used for cutting in a
young state, the growth renewing itself rapidly, and
the stakes being much used as props for vines in
a 'vinea.' We still grow it in this way as material
for fences.

The timber of full-grown trees was useful in building, but some Roman architects objected to its
excessive weight.

Flower, June.
Italian name, Castagno.

Cedrus

CEDRUS.

'odoratam stabulis accendere cedrum' (*Ge.* iii. 414).
'effigies . . . antiqua e cedro' (*Ae.* vii. 177).

The cedar of Lebanon was not known to the ancient Italians, and did not come to England until the year 1683, though it seems that before that the name was given to some other conifer. Virgil's tree is Juniperus oxycedrus, a native of central and western Italy, and is hardly more than a shrub, though it sometimes runs up to twelve feet. In early days wooden statues were made of it. The purpose of burning it in stables was to keep away snakes. Circe worked at her loom by the light of a fire of perfumed juniper (*Ae.* vii. 13). Virgil also couples the wood with cypress as building and other timber (*Ge.* ii. 443). The shrub refuses to grow satisfactorily in our climate.

Flower, February.
Italian name, Appeggi.

CEPA.

'cepa rubens . . . famem domat' (*Mor.* 83).

The onion, Allium cepa, is probably a native of Beluchistan, and had broken into several varieties before the time of Aristotle. Its Italian uses were much as ours. As a vegetable it was sometimes served in a thick fish-sauce.

Flower, June.
Italian name, Cipolla.

29

Trees, Shrubs, and Plants of Virgil

CERASUS.

'pullulat ab radice aliis densissima silva | ut cerasis'
(*Ge.* ii. 17).

Virgil makes no mention of the cherry which is indigenous in the woods of Italy. This is the gean, a tree without suckers, and with a dark and somewhat harsh fruit, from which is descended the morello. Virgil's cherry is Prunus cerasus, which produces many suckers, is rather a bush than a tree, and affords a red and juicy fruit. It is the origin of most of our cherries. The Romans held that it was introduced into this country by Lucullus in 73 B.C., but it seems never to have taken rank as a first-rate fruit. It was thought that they were best gathered with the morning dew on them. Eaten stone and all they were accounted a remedy for the gout.

Flower, April.
Italian name, Visciolo.

CERINTHA.

'cerinthae ignobile gramen' (*Ge.* iv. 63).

Honeywort (Cerinthe aspera) is a common plant in Italian fields and woody places, and is still called 'cerinta.' It is allied to our garden lungworts, and like some of them has leaves spotted with white. The flowers are yellow, with a purple base. Virgil joins it with balm as material for an ointment inducing a swarm of bees to settle in a hive.

The epithet applied to it is difficult, for in habit

30

Cerintha

and blossom the plant seems no more to deserve
it than many others which he names. It has been
explained as an allusion to the general distribution
of the plant, but this is unsatisfactory. It seems
possible that Virgil refers to the little account made
of honeywort in the works of the Greek botanists.
One is reminded of 'the little northern plant, long
overlooked,' which Linnaeus chose to bear his own
name.

> Flower, April and May.
> Italian names, Cerinta, Scarlattina, and Erba-
> tortora.

CICUTA.

'disparibus septem compacta cicutis | fistula' (*Ec.* ii. 36).
'fragili cicuta' (*Ec.* v. 85).

Umbelliferous plants are notoriously difficult to
identify, and Virgil may have used our word of any
plant of that type which Shakespeare and North-
amptonshire folk call kexes—any large plant of the
order with hollow stems. It seems likely that what
was used for executions at Athens was not hemlock
but cowbane, to which Linnaeus gave the name of
Cicuta virosa. This cannot well be Virgil's plant,
for it is rare in Italy, and confined to the lands north
of the Apennines. The Latin *cicuta* was, however,
a poisonous plant, and may well have been what we
call hemlock (Conium maculatum). If so, Linnaeus
has transposed the names, giving to hemlock the
Greek name for cowbane and to cowbane the Latin
name for hemlock.

Trees, Shrubs, and Plants of Virgil

Hemlock is found throughout Italy and Sicily. In a luxuriant state its stems would be too large for a pan-pipe, but the smaller stems were of the right size. Technically *cicuta* came to mean the piece of stem between two joints of reed.

The plant is sometimes six feet high, and may usually be recognized through the purple blotches on the smooth stem.

Flower, June and July.
Italian name, Cicuta.

COLOCASIUM.

' tellus | mixta . . . ridenti colocasia fundet acantho '
(*Ec.* iv. 20).

The caladiums, as our gardeners call them, of which Virgil's species is Colocasia antiquorum, the Indian taro, are akin to the arum or 'lords and ladies' of our woodlands. In Virgil's time they were grown in Egypt, and the esculent roots imported to Rome. They are not very good eating, and Dioscorides recommends boiling them to make them less sharp to the palate. According to Pliny, the large leaves were made into the drinking cups which Horace and Didymus call ' ciboria.' In later days the plant was introduced into Italy, but, except in the extreme south, it had to be protected with mats against hard weather. In Sicily it has established itself by the sides of streams.

Some of the American caladiums appear in state at the Royal Horticultural Society's shows, and have

32

a violent sort of beauty, which commends them to
the stoves of Dives, but they do not excite the envy
of a mere Corycian. They have, however, some
value in sub-tropical gardening.

Flower, spring.
Italian name, Colocasia.

CORIANDRUM.

'exiguo coriandra trementia filo' (*Mor.* 90).

Coriander (Coriandrum sativum) is an umbel-
laceous plant, a native of the East, and cultivated
in very early times for the sake of its seeds. These
seeds are mentioned in the Book of Exodus. They
were used medicinally and in cakes. The word
'filum' is used of the habit of a plant or possibly
of the stem. Our plant has a slender stem, and the
poet's description contrasts it with such stout kinsmen as 'ferula.'

Flower, May and June.
Italian name, Coriandola.

CORNUS.

'lapidosa . . . corna' (*Ae.* iii. 649 ; *Ge.* ii. 34).

The cornelian cherry (Cornus mas), near akin to
our dogwood, is a native of Greece and Italy. It
grows to the height of fifteen feet, and in March its
yellow flowers are conspicuous on the leafless boughs.
It seems to have been for the sake of its flowers that
it was first cultivated, for Theophrastus tells us that

the fruit of the wild form was sweeter and better. It is good for preserving, but in my garden is usually cut off by frost.

Virgil's epithet cannot mean more than that the fruit has a stone. He can hardly mean to speak ill of it, for he says, though here he must be in error, that it was sometimes grafted on the sloe. It is true that in our first passage the marooned Achaemenides complains that he had to live on 'victum infelicem, bacas lapidosaque corna'; but it must be remembered that he might regard even a fairly good fruit as unnourishing when it was his only food. The boy who plays the micher and eats blackberries, though he likes them well enough, would be sulky if on his coming home at night his mother said there was nothing in the stew-pot. Pliny, indeed, had no great fondness for cornels, for he says that they were dried in the sun, like prunes, just to show that there was nothing not created for man's belly.

In the early days of Rome the stem of the tree, 'bona bello cornus' (*Ge.* ii. 448), was made into a lance shaft. Hence in poetry 'cornus' sometimes means a lance (*Ae.* ix. 698, xii. 267). Better material, such as the ash, was afterwards employed. Usually the timber was too small for anything but wedges and the spokes of wheels. For these its hardness made it fit.

Flower, February.
Italian names, Corniolo and Crogniolo.

34

Corylus

CORYLUS.

> 'inter densas corylos' (*Ec.* i. 14).
> 'edurae coryli' (*Ge.* ii. 65).

The hazel, Corylus Avellana, gets its specific name from the Campanian town of Abella, where possibly the filbert was first grown. The slopes of Palestrina were also famous for nuts, which were therefore often called 'nuces Praenestinae.' Virgil makes no mention of the fruit, but Theophrastus compares its flavour to that of olive-oil.

The tree was grown for firewood, and in Tuscany you may still see women carrying home large faggots of it standing upright in baskets bound to their backs. Virgil forbids the planting of it among vines (*Ge.* ii. 299). The reason is that its roots spread and take much out of the soil. When the goat was sacrificed as an enemy to the vines (*ib.* 390), the spits on which the entrails were roasted were made of hazel wood, and it may be supposed that these spits also, as the product of an enemy to the vine, were afterwards consigned to the flames.

> Catkins, winter; female flower, March.
> Italian name, Nocciuolo.

CROCUS.

> 'crocum . . . rubentem' (*Ge.* iv. 182).
> 'picta croco . . . vestis' (*Ae.* ix. 614).

Of the crocus a dozen species are found in Italy, but Virgil's plant is only the saffron (Crocus sativus), which gets its name from an Arabic word

35

for yellow. The perianth of the flower is purplish, but the stigmata, from which the dye comes, are, as Martyn says, of the colour of fire. It must, I think, be to the stigmata that Virgil's epithet applies. The dye is too distinctly yellow, and a yellow blush would exceed even the ancient capacity for confounding colours.

As a native plant the saffron extends from Kurdistan to the Mediterranean, and some botanists regard it as a native of Italy. Arcangeli, however, says that it is only naturalized in his country, and Virgil seems to hold that opinion, for he says that the saffron perfume came from Tmolus, a range of mountains in Lydia. Theophrastus, however, holds that the best was made in Aegina and in Cilicia, but he adds that the plant was plentiful about Cyrene in North Africa. The Cilician brand was generally preferred at Rome.

The product of the stigmata had three uses: as a scent, as a dye, and as an ingredient in cookery. As a scent it is coupled in the Song of Solomon with spikenard, and at Rome mixed with wine it was used as a spray in the theatres and on the floors of rooms. It was also put into a pot-pourri. As a dye for clothing it was regarded as somewhat Oriental and luxurious. Virgil makes the fierce Numanus, a primitive Italian, taunt the followers of Aeneas with their yellow and purple robes: 'Vobis picta croco et fulgenti murice vestis' (*Ae.* ix. 614). Nevertheless, Virgil must often have seen women at least wearing it. For its abiding use in cookery

Crocus

we may refer to the clown in *The Winter's Tale*, who must have saffron, he says, to colour the warden pies, but nowadays it seems to be supplanted by cochineal.

Tennyson's line,

'And at their feet the crocus brake like fire,'

must refer to C. aureus, which is not found in Italy. It is the parent of our yellow crocuses. Our large purple crocuses come from C. versicolor, which grows in the hills by Nice and Mentone.

> Flower, autumn.
> Italian name, Zafferano.

CUCUMIS.

'tortus . . . per herbam | cresceret in ventrem cucumis'
(Ge. iv. 121).

The cucumber (Cucumis sativus) was of Eastern origin and in early cultivation, and a lodge in a garden of cucumbers is the Oriental equivalent of Tony Weller's pike. Virgil's phrase is precise.

Some kind of garden frame, 'speculare,' was used by Roman gardeners, but it is not clear whether as early as Virgil's time. Columella says that frames gave Tiberius his cucumbers in winter, and Martial (viii. 14) implies that these 'specularia' were no rarities under Domitan.

> Flower, summer.
> Italian name, Cetriolo.

Trees, Shrubs, and Plants of Virgil

CUCURBITA.

'gravis in latum demissa cucurbita ventrem' (*Mor.* 76).

The original country of the pumpkins and gourds is in some doubt. The kind named in our line is perhaps Cucurbita Pepo, which was brought from the Levant to England in the reign of Elizabeth. By Columella's time there were several varieties in Italy, perhaps some species and others hybrids. Pumpkins were cheap food, and an economical or niggardly entertainer could make of one fruit a dozen different dishes by cutting it into different shapes and cooking the sections in different ways.

> Flower, summer.
> Italian name, *Zucca.*

CUPRESSUS, OR CYPARISSUS.

'coniferae cyparissi' (*Ae.* iii. 680).
'Idaeis . . . cyparissis' (*Ge.* ii. 84).
'vittis atraque cupresso' (*Ae.* iii. 64).
'ferales . . . cupressos' (*Ae.* vi. 216).
'quantum lenta solent inter viburna cupressi' (*Ec.* i. 26).

The cypress (Cupressus sempervirens) seems to have travelled westward from the Taurus mountains, and Virgil may be right in taking it for a native also of the Caucasus (*Ge.* ii. 443). In speaking of cypresses of Ida (*ib.* 84) he seems to have in mind the belief of Theophrastus that the tree was native in Crete. In travelling by railway in Italy you may often descry on the hillside a square enclosed by cypresses, whose fastigiate growth makes

Cupressus, or Cyparissus

them easy to recognize at a considerable distance. The square is a cemetery, and you remember that Virgil's epithet for the tree is 'feralis' (*Ae*. vi. 216). The association of the cypress with funerals seems to be unexplained, for we can hardly accept Varro's view that the trees sheltered the mourners from the smell of the burning body. The timber was used in house-building (*Ge*. ii. 443).

The cypress is probably a long-lived tree. When Mrs. Piozzi visited the famous garden at Verona in the year 1785 she asked how old the cypresses were, and was told between four and five hundred years. On visiting the garden some twenty years ago I put the same question to the custodian and received the same answer. To such consistency as this a changeable mortal can but make a humble bow.

The meaning of 'coniferae,' as applied to our tree, was disputed by the ancient commentators. Some were for the obvious sense of cone-bearing. The cones of the cypress, which are about an inch in diameter, though less arresting than those of a fir, are distributed over the whole tree. Other authorities, pointing to Ovid's 'metas imitato cupressus,' considered Virgil to mean that the leafy part of the tree was shaped like the turning-post in a chariot race.

The cypress was sometimes grown to support vines. In that case it was recommended to plant the vine at some distance from the tree and train it accordingly.

Flower, April.

Italian name, Cipresso.

Trees, Shrubs, and Plants of Virgil

CYTISUS.

'florentem cytisum' (*Ec.* i. 78, ii. 64).
'sic cytiso pastae distendant ubera vaccae' (*Ec.* ix. 31).
'nec cytiso saturantur apes' (*Ec.* x. 30).
'tondentur cytisi' (*Ge.* ii. 431 ; cf. *Ge.* iii. 394).

Virgil's plant (Medicago arborea) is not wild in the Cisalpine, and he probably made his first acquaintance with it in the poems of Theocritus. In Sicily it is somewhat common, and Theocritus mentions it as food for goats. The plant, however, is a native of Tuscany, and, as it was evidently considered valuable, it may have been cultivated in Virgil's country. It is a tallish shrub, akin to the clovers. Virgil's epithet seems to imply that as food for goats it is best in the flowering season, which is from May to July. Theophrastus says that it is destructive even to trees, and it seems to have hungry roots.

The fourth passage suggests that, as cattle and goats are fond of the plant, farmers do well to grow it.

Flower, May to July.

[I have never heard and cannot find any Italian name for this plant. The name of *citiso* has been transferred to the laburnum.]

DICTAMNUM.

'dictamnum . . . puberibus caulem foliis et flore comantem | purpureo' (*Ae.* xii. 412).

Here we have a plant which Virgil can hardly have seen, and whose description he took from others. The plant is Origanum dictamnus, a little shrub with pink flowers, which is akin to marjoram. The leaves, as Virgil says, are covered with thick wool. Theophrastus was informed that they spoke truth who said that if goats ate it when they had been shot it ejected the arrow. With more truth Pliny says that the leaves had some power to cure wounds.

The plant was brought from Crete to England in the reign of Edward VI., but our winters are too hard for it, and it is not in general cultivation.

> Flower, summer.
> Italian name, Dittamo.

EBULUS.

> 'sanguineis ebuli bacis' (*Ec.* x. 27).

The danewort, or dwarf elder (Sambucus ebulus), is a very common weed in Italy, and still bears the name of *ebbio*. It is rather like the elder, but is an herbaceous plant, not a tree. The reddish-black berries give a blue dye, but their colour, when smeared on fresh, might be called red. It is said that statues of Pan were painted red.

The plant has established itself here and there in England, whither legend says it was brought by the Danes. It is supposed to have been used by them like woad as a dye for the human skin.

> Flower, June.
> Italian names, Ebbio, Lebbio, and Colore.

Trees, Shrubs, and Plants of Virgil

ERUCA.

'venerem revocans eruca morantem' (*Mor.* 85).

This little cruciferous plant, though called rocket in some books, really has no English name. In actual use the name of rocket is applied to some species of brassica and hesperis. Our plant is Eruca sativa, which in early spring bears a whitish flower tinged with violet. It grows in fields and open places, and its leaves are gathered for use in salads. In this country it seems not to be in cultivation.

> Flower, February to May.
> Italian names, Rucola and Ruchetta.

ERVUM.

'quam pingui macer est mihi taurus in ervo' (*Ec.* iii. 100).

This species of vetch, Vicia ervilia, is closely akin to the lentil, but its flowers are pinkish, while those of the lentil are white and smaller. Unlike the lentil, it is regarded as a native of Italy, and is cultivated there as fodder for cattle.

> Flower, June.
> Italian names, Mochi, Capogirlo, and Zirlo.

FABA.

'vere fabis satio' (*Ge.* i. 215 ; cf. *Ge.* i. 74).

On the season for sowing the field bean (Vicia faba) Virgil is not at one with the ancient Italian authorities, who commend October or November.

Faba

But Virgil was a Gaul, and in the land of the Po the bean was sown in February.

Italian botanists believe the bean to be of Asiatic origin, while other authorities hold that it was developed from some native vetch. In Sicily the young seeds are regarded as a fruit and eaten raw, the outer skin being first removed.

Virgil recommends that in the rotation of crops wheat should follow beans, 'laetum siliqua quassante legumen.' The advice is sound, for it is now known that leguminous plants have the property of fixing the nitrogen of the air.

The meaning of 'siliqua quassante' is disputed. I believe Martyn to be right in seeing a reference to the method of threshing beans. The halms are laid on the edge of the threshing-floor, and pushed across it by the feet of three or four men, who as they go beat the halm with sticks. The beans drop on to the floor, the halm is bundled at the other end of the floor, and winnowing is needless.

Beans were ground into meal, on which swine and other beasts were fed. As food for man it took the lowest rank, though it seems to have been frequently eaten by artisans.

Flower, April to June.

Italian name, Fava..

FAGUS.

'patulae recubans sub tegmine fagi'
(*Ec.* i. 1 ; cf. *Ec.* ii. 3, iii. 37, ix. 9; *Ge.* i. 173, ii. 71).

This name is etymologically identical with beech, and in Latin and English keeps its meaning, which,

43

if it be connected with φαγεῖν, refers to the esculent mast. In Greek the name was transferred to the Valonia oak.

The beech (Fagus silvatica) is native to a triangular region of which the points are Cilicia, Spain, and Norway. Theophrastus says that in Latium the beeches were splendid, and from them was named the spur of the Esquiline called Fagutal. Virgil's epithet is well illustrated by the great tree at Knowle with its diameter of over a hundred feet.

The wood is used for carpentry and carpenter's tools and for bowls and cups. Menalcas prizes the beechen cups carved by Alcimedon, possibly a friend of Virgil, whom he took this occasion to compliment (*Ec.* iii. 37). When Cowley and Wordsworth speak of the beechen bowl as characteristic of country life, they probably follow Virgil, for in England the maple was mostly used for this work. The fruit or mast of the tree is included under the name of 'glans,' which also covers the fruit of all oaks. The strength of the timber causes Virgil to recommend the use of it for the staff of the plough. Thin planks of it can, however, be bent, and thus it was the usual wood for making the circular bookcases called 'scrinia.'

Groups of beech-trees were sometimes allowed to stand until the trees were old and as timber worthless. We may hope that the love of beauty was in part the cause of this uneconomic course, and regret that it now has less force in Italy. Although Virgil habitually blends Sicilian and Cisalpine scenery, it looks as though 'the old beeches, now broken tops,' of the ninth Eclogue were a landmark on his Mantovan estate. Against this view it must be admitted that nowadays the tree does not descend to so low a level above sea. The shepherd in the fifth Eclogue disfigures a young beech by cutting his song on it, words and tune, and Gallus in the tenth may be supposed to use the same tree for his

> 'Woeful ballads
> Made to a mistress' eyebrow.'

Beech bark could be used as writing material, and some editors think that the shepherd so used it.

Flower, April.
Italian name, Faggio.

FAR.

'robusta . . . farra (*Ge.* i. 219).
'flava . . . farra' (*ib.* 73).
'farre pio . . .' (*Ae.* v. 745).
'mola . . . testatur deos' (*Ae.* iv. 517).
'adorea liba' (*Ae.* vii. 109).

Spelt (Triticum spelta) is an inferior variety of wheat (T. vulgare). The legend that wheat was the invention of Osiris may perhaps mean that wheat was developed from spelt in Egypt. Spelt was the original corn of the Romans, and was never supplanted by wheat in ceremonial and sacrificial use. Hence 'confarreatio' was the original and remained the most binding form of marriage. The grain was called 'ador,' and the cakes made of it had associations like those of our pancakes and hot-cross buns.

45

Trees, Shrubs, and Plants of Virgil

Coarsely ground, partly roast, and mixed with salt, it was called *mola*, and used in sacrifices and incantations (*Ec.* viii. 84). In our third passage Virgil, like Horace, uses 'far' in the sense of *mola*. From the latter comes the verb 'immolo,' to sacrifice.

Spelt is still cultivated in Italy on soils where wheat fails. The covering of the grain is as adhesive as that of barley.

The 'donatio adorea' was in old agricultural Rome the reward of a soldier for gallantry. Thus 'adorea' came to mean victory, and is so used in a fine line by Horace, who calls the day of Metaurus that

'qui primus alma risit adorea.'

Like other esculent grasses, spelt broke into several varieties. The best and whitest was grown about Chiusi, but another white kind gave a heavier crop. The kind called 'rutilum' had of course a reddish grain, and was held in less account.

Italian name, Spelta.

FERULA.

'florentes ferulas et grandia lilia' (*Ec.* x. 25).

This splendid umbelliferous plant (Ferula communis), though not very common in Italy, is widely distributed over the lower altitudes. The dark green and finely divided leaves make a fine mound in spring, and the flowering stem rises to six feet and in cultivation much more. It was held that this stem was the means by which Prometheus con-

Ferula

veyed fire from heaven, and the pith of it is still used as tinder. Like the lily, it is in flower from May to July. It grows well in our gardens, though the earliest leaves are apt to be damaged by frost, and it becomes a little ragged before the summer is gone.

Pan's garland in our passage is one which a man of little courage would hardly wear, but a god had the appropriate stature. Images of Silvanus represent as large a chaplet.

In a dried state the stem was the school cane, the mildest instrument of corporal punishment, the climax being ferula, scutica, flagellum. It was also an old man's walking-stick, and, if it was so used in Greece, perhaps ought to supplant the clouded cane in the Westminster Play.

> Flower, April to June.
> Italian name, Ferula.

FILIX.

'filicem curvis invisam . . . aratris' (*Ge.* ii. 189).

The bracken (Pteris aquilina) was as common in Italy as it is with us. The stout rhizomes go very deep and increase very fast. Though a modern plough would make little of them, they could doubtless be an obstacle to that which Virgil describes, and which is still used in the backward districts of southern Italy.

Bracken was useful as litter for sheep (*Ge.* iii. 297) and probably also for cattle, as it still is in Sussex

47

and other parts of England. Pliny says that the rhizomes were given to swine to fatten them.

Italian name, Felce aquilina.

FRAGUM.

'humi nascentia fraga' (*Ec.* iii. 92).

The wild strawberry (Fragaria vesca) is abundant in the hilly districts of Italy and Sicily. Although the large strawberry had been developed before Linnaeus assigned the specific name to our plant, it seems not to have been a Roman plant. The fruit of the wild kind was valued below its merits. Of all table fruits it grew closest to the ground.

Flower, April and May.
Italian names, Fragola and Fravola.

FRAXINUS.

'fraxinus in silvis pulcherrima' (*Ec.* vii. 65).
'ingens | fraxinus' (*Ge.* ii. 65).
'fraxineae . . . trabes' (*Ae.* vi. 181).

The ash (Fraxinus excelsior) deserves Virgil's epithet and its specific name, for it out-towers the manna ash, and is sometimes nearly a hundred feet high.

The timber had many uses. Poles of the younger growth were used as supports for vines.

The leaves, like those of the elm, were habitually stripped as food for cattle (*Ec.* ix. 60), as they still

Fraxinus

are in some parts of northern England. In Italy the hot summers often cause a lack of herbage.

Flower, March and April.
Italian name, Frassina.

FRUMENTUM.

Ge. i. 134, 150, 176, 189, ii. 205, iii. 176 ; *Ae.* iv. 406.

This is a general name for corn, especially spelt and wheat, and when used without qualification usually means wheat. Etymologically the word seems to stand for frugimentum, and so is connected with frux, fruor, fructus, and fruit.

GENISTA.

'lentae . . . genistae' (*Ge.* ii. 12).
'humiles . . . genistae' (*ib.* 434).

The fine yellow flowers of the Spanish broom (Spartium junceum) have long been an ornament to our gardens. It is common in southern Italy, and and is found also in the north. It grows on the plains and on dry and stony river banks. Virgil counts it among bee plants. The rush-like and almost leafless branches were used for withs to tie up bundles and stalked fruits. Pliny adds that it yields a yellow dye like its near kinsman, the dyer's greenweed, which abounds in the Weald of Sussex. Since the shrub grows to the height of eight feet, a group of it might afford shade to the shepherd, as it does in our second passage.

It is possible that the name may include also

the common broom (Cytisus scoparius), which is common in the lower ground of Italy, and especially magnificent round the ruins of Veii. It is highly probable that it also includes the dyer's greenweed (Genista tinctoria), which must certainly be the plant of the 'Pervigilium Veneris.' All leaves have flowers like enough in shape and colour to justify the Romans in giving them one generic name.

Flower, April to July.

Italian names: Ginestra and Maggio (Spartium).

Amareccioli, Estrici, Ruggiulo, and Ginestra de' Carbonaj (Cytisus).

Baccellina, Braglia, Cerretta, and Ginestrella (Genista).

HARUNDO.

'fluvialis harundo' (*Ge.* ii. 414).
'hic viridis tenera praetexit harundine ripas | Mincius'
(*Ec.* vii. 12).
'harundine glauca' (*Ae.* x. 205).
'agrestem tenui meditabor harundine Musam' (*Ec.* vi. 8).
'letalis harundo' (*Ae.* iv. 73).

Under this name there seem to be included two species, Phragmites communis, the common reed, and Arundo donax, the great reed. The former covers large tracts of ground in most temperate and some tropical regions, and it is a frequent fringe to river banks. When Virgil calls his river green he may be thinking not only of the banks but of the

Harundo

reflection of the reeds in the water. The reddish panicle of the reed turns grey in autumn, as is implied in our third passage.

Of the reed could be made pan-pipes and the shafts of arrows. Plautus and other writers refer to the use of it as thatch. Pliny seems to say that it was so used mainly in the north, while other authorities give the bulrush as the plant used for this purpose in the south.

There were other uses for which the great reed was more in demand. It formed the middle bar in the loom, not, as some lexicons give it, the comb. Pens were made of it and probably also thatch. The long stems were used as supports for vines, for knocking down olives which were too high on the tree to be gathered by hand, and for fishing-rods. Plashed alleys and pergolas were sometimes constructed of it. For these purposes it is still cultivated in Italy. In the warmer parts of England it succeeds in gardens, but on cold soils it cannot bear our frosts.

Flower, August and September.
Italian names: Canna (Arundo).
Canna di palude (Phragmites).

Trees, Shrubs, and Plants of Virgil

HEDERA, OR EDERA.

'hederae nigrae' (*Ge.* ii. 258).
'hedera pallente' (*Ec.* iii. 39; cf. *Ge.* iv. 124).
'hedera formosior alba' (*Ec.* vii. 38).
'errantes hederas' (*Ec.* iv. 19).
'hedera crescentem ornate poetam'
(*Ec.* vii. 25 ; cf. *Ec.* viii. 13).

The ivy (Hedera helix) as an evergreen was sacred
to Bacchus, and, since wine was a source of in-
spiration, became one of the emblems of the poet.
Virgil claims it especially for the woodland poet,
who does not claim rank with Homer or Pindar.
He hopes that Pollio will place his protégé's spray
of ivy among his own victorious bays. The berries
of the common ivy are black, but those of a rare
variety, H. chrysocarpa, are yellow, and Pliny says
that these were preferred for the poet's crown.
Virgil implies that the Corycian grew this variety in
his garden. According to Arcangeli, it grows in the
Neapolitan district and near Rome and Florence.
The gardener may have got it from Naples, whether
for the sake of its rarity and beauty or to give honey
to his bees. As it does not flower until September,
it would perhaps not be very valuable for the latter
purpose. Columella, however, says that ivy supplies
bees with very much honey, though it is not of the
best quality. It may be doubted whether Virgil
when he wrote the Eclogues had yet seen the yellow
fruited variety. He probably owed his knowledge of
it to Theocritus.

It is difficult to see why Virgil reckoned the

presence of ivy as a sign of a wickedly cold soil. In such ground ivy flourishes, as may be seen in the deep clay of some of our woodlands. It is true that it flourishes as vigorously on limestone and other warm soils.

Theophrastus says that dry sticks of ivy are the best for lighting a fire, and they are. To obtain the sacred spark of fire the Romans recommend the rubbing of a piece of bay wood on a piece of ivy.

Flower, September.
Italian names, Edera and Ellera.

HELLEBORUS.

'helleboros . . . graves' (*Ge.* iii. 451).

The plant of which Virgil gives the Greek name had also a Latin name, which Linnaeus gave to the genus. Our species is lyngwort (Veratrum album). Visitors of the Apennines and the Alps are struck by its large plaited leaves and liliaceous spike of flowers or, in August, of seeds, and it sometimes figures in our gardens. The poisonous qualities of the thick rhizome were well known to the ancients, though Lucretius and Pliny, while admitting that this was mortal to man, held that the leaves were fattening to goats. From my own observation I should say that they are always left uncropped. A decoction of the rhizome was accounted a cure for madness. The recipe for it was possessed by the inhabitants of Anticyra, an island in the Malian gulf. Hence Horace's 'naviget Anticyram' is a suggestion that his man is mad. Theophrastus, however, held that the best variety grew on Mount Oeta. Virgil, whose epithet refers to the poisonous quality of the plant, recommends its use in a sheep-dip, which by competent authorities is held to be a very good one. Modern gardeners use the pow-dered rhizome to kill caterpillars.

> Flower, June and July.
> Italian names, Veladro and Elabro bianco.

HIBISCUM.

> 'haedorum . . . gregem viridi compellere hibisco'
> > (*Ec.* ii. 30).
> 'gracili fiscellam texit hibisco' (*Ec.* x. 71).

From Dioscorides and Theophrastus we find that our plant had three names: one that used by Virgil, another that adopted by Linnaeus, while the third was wild mallow. We call it the marsh mallow (Althaea officinalis), and find it in sea marshes of southern England. Its light pink flowers much resemble those of its kinsmen, the mallows. The flowering stem is sometimes four feet high, and could be used as a wand in driving kids. It yields a long and strong fibre, out of which the shepherd in our second passage weaves a pliant basket, such as we use for carrying fish. Virgil sometimes uses an adjective where we use a noun. As he writes 'tenue aurum,' meaning threads of gold, so here he writes 'gracili hibisco,' meaning fibre of mallow.

Holus

The basket would serve for letting whey out of curdled milk.

> Flower, May to July.
> Italian names, Altea, Benefisci, and Malvaccione.

HOLUS.

'rarum . . . holus' (*Ge.* iv. 130).

This is a general name for kitchen garden stuff, and 'holitor' was a greengrocer. Virgil's epithet means that the plants were set in rows.

In Italy, especially in the south, vegetables play a larger part in the people's diet than with us. The volcanic soil round Naples grows them excellently, and in Taranto I have seen a heap of lettuce eight feet high. Virgil names endive, celery, garlic, cucumber, and caladium. Among others that he must have known would be cabbage, turnip, lettuce, nettle, onion, and globe artichoke. One of them might be alexanders, whose bright green leaves are conspicuous on the Dover cliffs. Little more than a century ago Abercrombie gave directions for growing and blanching it, but it has now dropped out of use. Having tried it, I can hardly say that it deserved a better fate.

HORDEUM.

'fragili . . . hordea culmo' (*Ge.* i. 317 ; cf. *ib.* 210).

Barley (Hordeum vulgare) was probably of Eastern origin, and must have come early into cultivation. In Palestine it was made into bread, and the κριθινὸς

55

οἶνος, which Xenophon came across in Asia, must have been some kind of ale. The Greeks held that barley bread strengthened the senses, and especially the eyesight.

Pearl barley was made into a coarse porridge called 'polenta,' a name afterwards transferred to the finer porridge made of ground chestnuts, and now used of the porridge made of maize. Pliny, if his text be right, implied that the finer porridge made of lentil meal was the earlier use of Italy, and that they took the coarser porridge from the Greeks, whose word for it is χονδρός.

Barley was given to mules as we give oats to horses, but draught cattle were said to have no liking for it.

Virgil accepts the Greek belief that barley, if ill cultivated, would degenerate into darnel (*Ec.* v. 36). His epithet contrasts the stem with the stronger stem of wheat.

Italian name, Orzo.

HYACINTHUS AND VACCINIUM.

'suave rubens hyacinthus' (*Ec.* iii. 63).
'ferrugineos hyacinthos' (*Ge.* iv. 183).
'latus niveum molli fultus hyacintho' (*Ec.* vi. 53).
'ille comam mollis iam tondebat hyacinthi' (*Ge.* iv. 137).
'vaccinia nigra leguntur' (*Ec.* ii. 18).
'et nigrae violae sunt et vaccinia nigra' (*Ec.* x. 39).

It seems probable that 'vaccinium' is the Latin form of ὑάκινθος, and in our last passage it takes its place, Virgil following the line of Theocritus,

Hyacinthus and Vaccinium

καὶ τὸ ἴον μέλαν ἐστὶ καὶ ἁ γραπτὰ ὑάκινθος.

Pliny's 'vaccinium' is an entirely different plant. He calls it a shrub, and it may possibly be the bilberry.

No ancient flower has stirred more controversy than this, and it cannot be said that the identification even now is beyond dispute. Columella has caused some complication by speaking of hyacinths not only as 'ferrugineos,' wherein he merely followed Virgil, but also as 'vel niveos vel caeruleos' and as 'caelestis luminis.' We may, however, leave out of account this sky-blue hyacinth, possibly the two-leaved squill, for beyond doubt it is not the same plant as Virgil's. It may, however, be well to bear in mind that the Greeks applied the name to several flowers, which do not greatly resemble each other, and that probably among them are the squill, already mentioned, the larkspur, and the flower which we know as the hyacinth.

Let us start with the passage of Ovid in which, as Martyn says, 'the form of the hyacinth is particularly described.' The poet is describing what followed the death of the youth Hyacinthus:

> 'Ecce cruor, qui fusus humi signaverat herbam,
> Desinit esse cruor, Tyrioque intentior ostro
> Flos oritur formamque capit quam lilia, si non
> Purpureus color his, argenteus esset in illis.
> Non satis hoc Phoebost, is enim fuit auctor honoris.
> Ipse suos gemitus foliis inscribit, et ai ai
> Flos habet inscriptum, funestaque litera ductast.'

Now, if this passage contained all our information, there could be no doubt about our plant. There

is only one Italian species so near to the white lily
as to justify Ovid's word. This is Lilium bulbiferum,
with its variety, as Arcangeli ranks it, L. croceum,
which the Romans are not likely to have distinguished from the type. The figures in Curtis's
Botanical Magazine (L. candidum 278, L. bulbiferum 1018, and L. croceum, given with a wrong
name, 36) show the likeness of these plants in habit
and perianth. The objection that nothing very like
letters can be found on them applies, I believe,
equally to any other Italian lily. I cannot resist
the conclusion that Ovid meant what our forefathers
called the red lily.

It does not, however, follow that Virgil's plant
is the same as Ovid's. Martyn supposed himself
to find both in the purple martagon, L. martagon
(*B.M.*, 893). He sinks, as Johnson would have
said, the wide differences between this plant and
the white lily. In the latter the perianth is erect
and its divisions but little reflexed, while the martagon belongs to the Turk's-cap group, in which the
perianth is cernuous, and its divisions very much
reflexed. The stem leaves of the martagon are in
distant whorls, while those of the white lily are
irregular and even crowded. It is hard to believe
that the martagon is Ovid's plant.

On the question of colour Virgil does not give us
much help, for his 'suave rubens' and 'ferrugineus'
have too wide a range. He applies both to the dye
of the Tyrian shell-fish. The ram in the fourth
Eclogue has his fleece coloured 'suave rubenti

Hyacinthus and Vaccinium

murice,' and in the Aeneid (xi. 772) the priest Chloreus is described as 'peregrina ferrugine clarus et ostro,' a phrase which must be taken as hendiadys. The Tyrian dye was probably both red and purple, and 'rubens' will cover both; while 'ferrugineus,' which is applied to objects of less cheerful hue, such as Charon's boat (*Ae.* vi. 303) and the gloom in the sky after Caesar's death (*Ge.* i. 467), not only covers both but includes the tint of a dull and lowering purple. That 'fulgor' is ascribed to the hyacinth (*Ae.* xi. 70) is rather against the martagon.

Last comes the matter of the inscription. In our last passage Virgil omits the γραπτά of his original, but he has a reference to it in the shepherd's riddle (*Ec.* iii. 106),

> 'Dic quibus in terris inscripti nomina regum
> Nascantur flores,'

to which the answer seems to be Αἴας, who is Ajax. Martyn says that on the martagon the dark spots run together in such a manner as to form the letters AI, 'which,' he naïvely adds, 'I have caused to be represented in the figure.' It seems clear that these marks had not run together on the specimen supplied to Cole, who drew the illustration, for the addition is stiff and unnatural. It may be compared with Sowerby's figure in *English Botany,* where the dark marks are drawn naturally. I grew the martagon as a boy and I grow it now, and never in half a century have I seen on it anything like the letters which our good professor 'caused to be represented.'

Trees, Shrubs, and Plants of Virgil

One objection that may be made to the claim of the martagon applies equally to the red lily, if its old name may still be used. It seems that neither of them grows wild in Sicily. It is of course possible that they become extinct, but in the case of the martagon this is unlikely. As Mr. A. Grove says in his monograph on the genus, it is the one lily that will grow wherever the seed happens to fall. In a copse at Mickleham it has so completely established itself, southerner though it is, as to obtain admittance to the English flora. It seems unlikely that the martagon can be the written hyacinth of Theocritus.

There is, moreover, a Sicilian flower the inside of whose perianth bears marks, which do frequently take the form of an A, with a smaller blotch after it, which one could plausibly 'cause to be represented' as an I. This is the corn-flag (Gladiolus segetum). Of many specimens which I gathered near Selinunte and near Catania almost all had marks, and about one in five had the marks described above. A figure of a kindred species, G. communis, is given in *English Botany*, but this has no marks that resemble letters. It is against the corn-flag's claim and somewhat in favour of the martagon's that the shepherds in Theocritus seek the hyacinth in the hills.

> Flower: Lilies, July and August.
> Corn-flags, April to July.
>
> Italian names: Giglio Rosso (Lilium bulbiferum).

Intubum

Italian names : Spaderello, Coltellaccio, Pan-
caciolo (Gladiolus).
Martagone (Lilium marta-
gon).

INTUBUM.

'amaris intuba fibris' (*Ge.* i. 120).
'potis gauderent intuba rivis' (*Ge.* iv. 120).

There is some uncertainty about this plant, but it
is probably endive, and some botanists hold that
endive is a cultivated form of Cichorium divaricatum,
a Mediterranean plant which is a rare native of
Italy. It is a salad plant, and being harder than
lettuce is of special value in the winter. It is best
blanched, since otherwise the bitterness of the leaves
is excessive. The same bitterness is found in the
root, and Columella may refer to the root or to the
leaves when he says that it is a stimulant to a torpid
palate. The plant is closely allied to succory or
chicory, of which various forms are grown both for
the root and for the blanched leaves. The form
of endive mostly grown in our gardens is said to
have been produced in China.

Flower, April to June.
Italian name, Endivia.

ILEX.

'ilice sub nigra' (*Ec.* vi. 54).
'sub arguta . . . ilice' (*Ec.* vii. 1).
'opaca | ilice' (*Ae.* vi. 208 ; cf. *Ae.* xi. 851).

The holm or holly-oak (Quercus ilex) is one of the
finest of Italian trees. There is a magnificent line

of them along the Galleria di sopra near Albano,
but the tree does not go high into the Apennines.
The leaves are much darker than those of the
common oak and usually untoothed, and the tree
is evergreen. In a wind there is a harsh rustling
in the leaves. The acorns, which are small but
plentiful (*Ge.* iv. 81), are food for swine (*Ge.* ii. 72 ;
Ae. iii. 390). The wood was used for making water-
troughs (*Ge.* iii. 330). Bees, says Virgil, sometimes
establish themselves in the body of a decaying holm-
oàk (*Ge.* ii. 453).

In England the tree has been grown since Elizabeth's time, and attains full stature, but is apt to
divide into two or more stems. Perhaps the finest
specimen is one in the town of Uckfield.

The gall, ' coccum,' which yields a scarlet dye,
seems to be most common on Q. coccifera, but our
ancient authorities say that it was also found on the
holm-oak.

> Flower, April and May.
> Italian name, Elice.

INULA.

' malvaeque inulaeque virebant ' (*Mor.* 73).

Elecampane (Inula Helenium) is found here and
there in Italy as in England, but appears to be
nowhere very common. My own plants generally
produce a few self-sown seedlings. It was cultivated
for its bitter root, which were used both as a table
vegetable and as a medical remedy. It was boiled

with vinegar. The plant is worth growing in rough
places for the sake of its large leaves and bold composite heads of yellow blossom, but it goes ragged
rather early.

> Flower, July and August.
> Italian name, Elenio.

JUNCUS.

'limoso . . . palus obducat pascua iunco' (*Ec.* i. 49).
'aliquid . . . quorum indiget usus | viminibus mollique
paras detexere iunco' (*Ec.* ii. 71).

Under this name are included our common plait-
ing rushes, Juncus effusus and J. conglomeratus, and
probably other species. Both kinds are too common
in the marshy lands round Mantova, and, although
the first Eclogue gives us a deliberate confusion of
Cisalpine and Sicilian scenery, it is probable that
Virgil's father had to fight against a weed which
cattle will not eat. In the passage of Theocritus
which Virgil follows the rushes are woven into
baskets. They were also used for making ropes,
the use of hemp fibre being unknown. Larger ropes
were made of flax.

> Flower, June and July.
> Italian name, Giunco.

JUNIPERUS.

> 'stant et iuniperi' (*Ec.* vii. 53).
> 'iuniperi gravis umbra' (*Ec.* x. 76).

The common juniper (Juniperus communis), as it
grows on the South Downs, is a somewhat scrubby

object, but in favourable positions becomes a shapely tree eighteen or twenty feet high. It is very common in Italy and attains this height in the lower country. It owes its name, which means Juno's pear, to its sweet and fragrant fruits, which do not ripen until the second summer. The seeds, which in later times flavoured gin, may also have been eaten.

The Italians have a proverb, 'Dove non viene il Sole, non viene la Santà.' This applies to the houses, and out of doors the hour after sunset, to which our second passage refers, is accounted un-healthy. I know no reason why the shade of the juniper should be accounted especially baneful.

> Flower, February to April.
> Italian names, Ginepro and Zinepro.

LABRUSCA : see VITIS.

LACTUCA.

'grata . . . nobilium requies lactuca ciborum ' (*Mor.* 76).

The lettuce (Lactuca sativa) is held by Italian botanists to have been developed out of their native species, L. scariola. In earlier Roman days it ended the meal, but afterwards was *hors d'œuvre* at the beginning, and was accounted an appetizer. As with us, lettuces were blanched. This, however, was done, not by tying up, but by putting stones on the plant, much as we treat endive. There were at least two varieties, of which one had a brownish leaf.

> Flower, July to October.
> Italian name, Lattuga.

Lappa and Tribulus

Lappa and Tribulus.
            'lappaeque tribulique' (*Ge.* i. 153, iii. 385).

It is clear from Pliny that 'lappa' is the ἀπαρίνη of Theophrastus, and it is clear that Theophrastus' plant is goose-grass or cleavers (Galium Aparine), and not burdock, as it figures in lexicons. Virgil might well recommend its extirpation where sheep were kept for wool. Not only the globular seed-heads but even the stems and leaves cling to a fleece. It was to protect the fine fleeces against cleavers as well as against marruca and other thorns that the Tarentine farmers clothed their sheep with coats of hide. Greek irony stamped its clinging way with the name of the philanthropic plant. With us it grows mostly in hedges and waste places, but Pliny notes that it was a pest in cornland.

In both our passages it is coupled with 'tribulus,' which is the star thistle (Centaurea calcitrapa). In this plant the involucral bracts end in long spines capable of doing much damage, and it owes its specific name to its likeness to a caltrop. The spines remain when the flower has faded, and made Pliny say that the plant is peculiar in that the fruit as well as the flower is spinous. The plant, common in Italy, occurs occasionally in southern England, as on the coast round Dover.

Flower: Lappa, April to September.

Tribulus, July and August.

Italian names: Speronella, Attacca-mani, At-
tacca-veste (Galium).

Calcatreppola, Ippofesto,
Ceceprete (Centaurea).

Trees, Shrubs, and Plants of Virgil

Laurus.

'Parnasia laurus' (*Ge.* ii. 18).
'virgulta sonantia lauro' (*Ae.* xii. 522).

In our gardens the name of laurel has been usurped by an evergreen cherry, which came from the Levant in the days of Charles II. The true laurel is the bay (Laurus nobilis), from which we get camphor and cinnamon. Associated with the legend of Daphne, its name in Greek, it became sacred to Apollo (*Ae.* iii. 82, 360). A soldier bore it in a triumph to indicate that he was sanctified from the pollution of blood. Sprays of it were burnt in incantations and to get omens from the crackling (*Ec.* viii. 83). It was also valued for its aromatic scent, and Corydon joins it in his nosegay with the myrtle (*Ec.* ii. 54). Virgil tells the farmer to gather the berries in the winter (*Ge.* i. 306); they yield a scented oil.

The bay is not uncommon in southern Italy, but I do not know any thickets of it such as are described in our second passage as victims of a forest fire. It is propagated by suckers (*Ge.* ii. 18).

Flower, March.
Italian name, Alloro.

Lens.

'Pelusiacae lentis' (*Ge.* i. 228).

The lentil (Vicia lens), a small blue-flowered vetch, was one of the first leguminous plants to be cultivated. Its native country is uncertain, but

66

Italian botanists think that Virgil may be right in assigning it to Egypt. Others hold that it was developed in Italy out of some other vetch with smaller and less valuable seeds. Ancient authorities agree with Virgil that it should be sown in November, but those who wish to grow it in England would do well to wait till March and choose a warm spot. In our climate it is of less value than the Dutch brown bean and other varieties of Phaselus which we owe to America. The seeds are imported in considerable quantities for use as a vegetable and in soup.

The turn of Virgil's phrase must imply either that lentils are of less value than corn or that their cultivation is so easy that a scientific farmer might leave it to less able hands.

Flower, July and August.
Italian names, Lente and Lenticchia.

LIGUSTRUM.

'alba ligustra cadunt' (*Ec.* ii. 18).

It were much to be desired that our English gardeners shared Corydon's contempt for the privet (Ligustrum vulgare), against which Mr. William Robinson has waged a righteous war almost in vain. The wretched shrub claims the power of resisting London smoke, and one is minded to wish that it could not. However much it is planted, perhaps no one chooses to gather its sickly smelling flowers. The shrub is closely akin to the olive and the ash, who, it must be allowed, do their best to hide their relationship to their ugly cousin. Regretfully I feel bound to quote Tennyson:

> 'A skin
> As clean and white as privet when it flowers.'

Martyn endeavoured to identify our plant with the great bindweed (Convolvulus sepium), whose large white and bell-shaped flowers adorn our hedges, and whose throttling stems are sometimes a pest in gardens. But this plant appears in Pliny under the name of convolvulus together with a synonymous worm or caterpillar, and it seems clear that Ligustrum was a shrub. It is a pity, for the flowers of the bindweed are much of a size with those of the red and white lilies, and, if 'hyacinthus' or 'vaccinium' be the red lily, Virgil's contrast is better than one between privet and martagons or corn-flags or aught else.

Flower of privet, June.
Italian name, Ligustro.

LILIUM.

'alba lilia' (*Ge.* iv. 130; *Ae.* xii. 69).
' candida lilia ' (*Ae.* vi. 709).
' florentes ferulas et grandia lilia ' (*Ec.* x. 25).

Lilium candidum, which some call St. Joseph's lily, is equally conspicuous in Italian paintings and in English cottage gardens, though of late a scoundrel fungus has done it much harm. It occurs sparingly in Italy, but may well have been more

68

Lilium

common in ancient days, and it is the only lily which is a native of Sicily. Virgil names it as a bee plant (*Ae.* vi. 709).

Flower, May to July.
Italian name, Giglio.

LINUM.

> 'urit enim campum lini seges' (*Ge.* i. 77).
> 'velati lino' (*Ae.* xii. 120).

The reading in the latter passage is doubtful, and many editors accept 'limo.'

The manufacture of linen dates back to prehistoric times. The earliest linen seems to have been made of flax supplied by the fibrous bark of Linum angustifolium, a native of the Mediterranean region and of north-west Europe. This plant is sometimes annual, sometimes perennial, but is inferior to L. usitatissimum, an annual, which was perhaps a native of Asia Minor, though now it seems to occur only in cultivation or as a relic of it. In Italy it seems to have been grown to no great extent and only for the oil of its seeds, linen being imported from the East. Another product of flax is cambric, and both this and linen were and are used in the vestments of priests. Fishing nets were made of the fibre (*Ge.* i. 142).

Virgil's observation that flax 'runs' the soil is confirmed both by ancient and by modern observation, and some of the Roman authorities would on that account dissuade farmers from growing it.

Columella in particular says it should be grown only in districts where it commands a high price.

The plant is sometimes grown in our gardens for its blue flowers, but in beauty it is excelled by L. Narbonense, a perennial, and a native of Liguria, Lombardy, and Corsica.

> Flower, April and May.
> Italian name, Lino.

LOLIUM.

> 'infelix lolium' (*Ec.* v. 37; *Ge.* i. 154).

Great poets often retain a sense of the original meaning of words, and here Virgil's epithet, which at first meant 'unsuckling,' evidently means 'un-feeding.' Lolium temulentum, the drunken darnel, as Linnaeus called it from its supposed effects, is a grass near akin to rye, and is the plant which the enemy in the parable sowed in the corn. It was an ancient superstition among farmers that in a bad season wheat seeds degenerated into darnel. The qualities of the plant have long been matter of dispute. Hooker describes it as very poisonous, but the seeds have often been eaten with impunity. It seems, however, to be liable to the attacks of a minute fungus, which either is poisonous itself or creates a toxic power in the host plant. In either condition it so affects the eyesight as to create one of the symptoms of intoxication. Arcangeli tells us that in Italy it grows everywhere in the corn. With us it is only a colonist and, though widely dis-

Lolium

tributed, nowhere a common plant.   It may be well
distinguished from rye-grass by its annual duration
and its long awns.

Italian name, Loglio.

LOTUS.

> ' genus haud unum . . . loto ' (*Ge.* ii. 83).
> ' lotos ' (*Ge.* iii. 394).

It was recognized by Theophrastus that many
plants called lotus had nothing in common but the
name, and our passages refer to very different
species.   The first is an enumeration of trees whose
genera have more than one species, and the tree
named is the nettle-tree (Celtis Australis).   Though
closely akin to the elm and the nettle, it has for its
fruit a blackish drupe the size of a pea.   Ovid and
Martial call it aquatic, but according to Arcangeli
its usual habitat is the debris of rocks.   It has
somewhat ovate leaves with pubescent under-
surfaces.   The wood was used for ' cardines '—that
is, the uprights to which the planks of a door were
fastened, and which seem to survive in the pin of
a hinge.   What tree Virgil classed with it there is
nothing to show.

The ' lotus ' of our second passage is described as
good food for milch ewes.   It probably covers
several species which still bear its name, and, if it
is the plant of Theophrastus, especially L. tenuis
and L. ubiginosus.   These are of the same genus
as the bird's-foot trefoil or butter-and-eggs of our

71

fields. This is commended as fodder by agricultural authorities, and some think that it is Virgil's plant. Martyn took it for the white water-lily, but it seems unlikely that this would be eaten by sheep, and Martyn was misled by the mention in Theophrastus of another 'lotus,' which has been identified with one of the Nile water-lilies, which is not found in Italy.

Flower: Celtis, April and May.
Lotus, May and June.
Italian names: Arcidiavolo, Spaccasassi, and Lotu (Celtis).
Mullaghera (Lotus).

LUPINUS, OR LUPINUM.

'tristis . . . lupini . . . fragiles calamos silvamque sonantem'
(*Ge.* i. 75).

The common lupin (Lupinus albus) is of uncertain origin, but is possibly wild in some parts of the northern Apennines, and has long been cultivated in the Mediterranean region.

The epithet of 'tristis' may refer to the slight bitterness of the seeds, but possibly implies a false etymology. Virgil may, in spite of the quantity of the vowel, have derived lupin from λύπη, pain. There can, however, be little doubt that the word must be classed with foxglove and harebell and the many plant names which come from beasts. It is the plant of 'lupus,' the wolf.

The lupin is grown both for the seeds and as fodder, and thus, as Pliny says, is eaten both by

Lupus, or Lupinum

man and by beast. Moreover, like other leguminous plants, it was grown for the manurial value of the nitrogen which it secretes. Palladius recommends sowing it in September and ploughing the crop in. It is still largely grown in Campania.

Virgil had observed that, when the crop is harvested, the seeds rattle in the large pod.

Our garden lupins are mostly American, and have been much hybridized and improved under cultivation.

Flower, April and May.
Italian name, Lupino.

LUTUM.

'aries . . . mutabit vellera luto' (*Ec.* iv. 43).

The common dyer's weed or weld (Reseda luteola) is to be found in many parts both of Italy and of England. It is nearly akin to mignonette and may be recognized by the likeness in flower and seed vessel. It yields a yellow dye, which is obtained by boiling the whole plant when in flower, though the colouring matter is strongest in the seeds. In commerce the dye is known as Dutch pink. Blue cloths dipped in it turn green.

Flower, May and June.
Italian names, Biondella and Guaderella.

MALUS.

The general word for fruit was 'poma.' This included 'mala,' the larger fleshy fruits, 'nuces,' all

73

nuts, and also what we call bush fruits and others, such as plums, for which there was no divisional name. Virgil uses 'malus' of three trees, two of them belonging to the natural order of Rosaceae and the third to Aurantiaceae, and possibly of a fourth.

A. Apple: Pyrus malus.

'mutatam . . . insta mala | ferre pyrum ' (*Ge*. ii. 34).
'steriles platani malos gessere valentes' (*ib*. 70).

These passages probably refer to the apple. In Italy it seems to bewray a foreign origin by its dislike for the hot summers. It could be grafted on the pear but not on the plane, to which it is not akin. The earliest apple was *museum* or *melimelum*, our summering, the best keeper the amerine.

B. Quince: Pyrus cydonia.

'malo me Galatea petit' (*Ec*. iii. 64).
'aurea mala' (*ib*. 71).

The former of these passages may refer to the apple, but, as the quince was sacred to Venus and the thrown apple is a challenge to love, it may well be the quince. Virgil took his phrase here from Theocritus. At Athens, as is pretty clear from Aristophanes, this method of making love was confined to Doll Tearsheet and her kind. A modern quince of the pear-shaped type would be a clumsy pellet in a girl's hand, but the fruit may well have grown larger under cultivation. The ancient authorities mention several varieties, and with us one is occasionally found which has an apple-shaped fruit.

Malus

The association of the quince with love was not destroyed by Christianity. It may be that the quinces, for which the Nurse in *Romeo and Juliet* said they were calling in the pantry, were appropriate to the impending marriage, though throwing them was out of fashion, and indeed Romeo had no need of missile hints.

The quince came westward by way of Crete, and its name is derived from κυδώνιον, the apple of Cydonis, the Cretan city.

There are other passages in Virgil of which we must say that he may have meant either apples or quinces or both. Such are the jilted lover's wish for an inverted world, 'mala ferant quercus' (*Ec.* viii. 54), and the reference to 'malifera Abella' (*Ae.* vii. 740), The town, now Avella Vecchia, is in Campania, and had a renown for nuts as well as for soft fruit. The fruit of the Hesperides (*Ec.* vi. 61) were probably thought of as quinces, and Ovid calls them 'aurea poma.' He also describes the leaves as 'fulva,' a poetic exaggeration, which shows that his fruit had in it a touch of the mythical.

The phrase 'roscida mala' has been variously interpreted. Conington and other editors, following Servius, see a reference to the morning dew, while others take the epithet to be specific of a distinct fruit. The former interpretation is supported by the phrase of Theocritus, τὰ ῥόδα τὰ δροσόεντα, and more decisively by the Roman belief, mentioned by Pliny, that some fruits were best gathered with the morning dew on them. Moreover, when Propertius

Trees, Shrubs, and Plants of Virgil

speaks of 'roscida poma' (I. xx. 36) he seems to mean fruits splashed by the fountain into which Hylas was drawn by the nymphs.

Of the phrase in *Ec.* ii. 51, 'cana legam tenera lanugine mala,' it is difficult to make anything. The editors say quinces, but this ignores 'cana.' There were, however, three varieties of the quince, and one of these may have had a more hoary skin than the chrysomela. Our own pear-shaped fruit has a lighter skin than the apple-shaped and the Portuguese varieties, both cultivated in this country. The peach, which Virgil's description might suit, seems to have been of later introduction.

C. Citron: Citrus medica (*Ge.* ii. 126-135).

The Latin name for the citron was usually Malus medica and sometimes Malus Persica, a use which has caused some confusion with the peach. Virgil's account of it is his one attempt to describe from literary sources a tree of which he can have seen only the imported fruit. The tree is of Persian origin, and one variety of it is well known as the West Indian lime, of which Mrs. Soorocks gave one withered specimen to Bailie Waft. Virgil took most of his description from Theophrastus, but adds one or two touches whose origin I have failed to trace. Moreover, his text had one corrupt word, which is correct in the extant manuscripts, but corrupted in some which were seen by Athenaeus, who mistook the corrupt for the correct.

The points which Virgil takes from Theophrastus

are that the tree is fragrant, that it is a remedy against poison, and that it sweetens the breath. The taste of the fruit probably came from his own observation, though it was not regarded as esculent. The points which he adds are that the leaves are not shaken off by the wind and that the petals are slow to drop. The point in which he followed the false reading in Theophrastus is the comparison of the leaves to those of the bay. The right reading is not δάφνης, the bay, as Virgil and Athenaeus found it in their copies, but ἀνδράχλης. This is Arbutus Andrachne, a Greek tree with oblong and blunted leaves like the citron's, whereas the leaves of the bay are acute. Thus Virgil's mistake enables us to restore to his copy of Theophrastus a reading not found in the extant manuscripts and not correct.

From Theophrastus and Macrobius we may add that the fruit was placed among clothes to protect them from moths, and Macrobius ventures to surmise that Homer's θυώδεα Ϝείματα owed their scent to the citron.

In Imperial times the citron was grown in Italy, but in winter it was necessary to protect the trees with mats stretched over pillars as lemon-trees are now protected at Salò on the Lake of Garda.

> Flower of Apple and Quince, May.
> Italian names: Melo (apple); Cotogno (Quince); Cedro (Citron).

Trees, Shrubs, and Plants of Virgil

MALVA.

'Malvaeque inulaeque virebant' (*Mor.* 73).

Of the eight species of mallow native to Italy more than one may be included under this name, but it is chiefly applied to our common roadside plant, Malva silvestris. The leaves of it were used as a salad and a pot-herb, and were accounted among the most digestible of foods. The Greeks did not eat it uncooked. English children are fond of the nutty unripe seeds, which from their shape are called cheeses, but I know no evidence of a like fondness in Italy. Horace, if the stanza be not spurious, couples mallow with chicory as the food of a man of simple tastes.

Flower, March to October.
Italian name, Malva.

MEDICA (*Ge.* i. 215).

Lucern (Medicago sativa) appears to be native on dry banks in the Apennines, though according to Hooker it is known only in cultivation. He suggests that it may be a cultivated form of M. falcata, a yellow-flowered medick which has established itself in East Anglia. The flower of lucern is blue or purple. Its name of Μηδική refers to a supposed Persian origin of the plant, but I do not find that it occurs in Asia either wild or cultivated. It is still the chief fodder crop in some parts of Italy. The plant is perennial and was sometimes allowed to stand for ten years. It had the further value that it

Medica

could be mown six times or in favourable seasons
even ten times a year.

Flower, May to September.

Italian name, Erba Medica.

MELISPHYLLUM.

'adsperge . . . trita melisphylla' (*Ge.* iv. 63).

Balm (Melissa officinalis) is a labiate plant, native
in Italy and long in cultivation. It has a scent like
that of the citron. Virgil enjoins the mixing of its
pounded leaves with honeywort to induce bees to
swarm, and it is still sometimes used in the South
of England to smear on a skep. The plant supplies a tonic oil which at one time was much used
in drink for a sick person. Largely grown for this
purpose it has naturalized itself here and there in
southern England. Its scent is like that of the
sweet verbena (Aloysia citriodora). Anne Page bids
her elves scour the chairs of Windsor Castle with
juice of balm, and the plant was common in the
monastic gardens of the Middle Ages.

Flower, July to September.

Italian names, Appiastro, Cedronella, and
Citraggine.

MILIUM.

'milio venit annua cura' (*Ge.* i. 216).

Millet (Panicum miliaceum) came from the East,
but probably, unlike wheat, not from the great
plains, for it does better on hilly ground, and can

79

Trees, Shrubs, and Plants of Virgil

withstand much drought. It is still cultivated in Italy in dry and hilly fields. It will be remembered that it is one of the six components of the bread of which, according to Ezekiel (iv. 9), the Israelites were to eat for three hundred and ninety days.

Italian name, Miglio.

MORUS.

'sanguineis frontem moris et tempora pingit' (*Ec.* vi. 22).

The black mulberry (Morus nigra) is an Asiatic tree, which was early in cultivation, and may well be the tree in whose tops King David was to hear the sound of marching. It came into England in the reign of Edward VI. The colour of the berries is near enough to that of blood to justify Virgil's epithet, and indeed is ascribed by Ovid to the blood of Pyramus, who killed himself under a mulberry, as he does in *A Midsummer-Night's Dream*.

The word 'morum' is applied to other like berries, such as the blackberry. In modern Italy the name of 'moro' has been transferred to the white mulberry, whose fruit is a very pale red. This was a tree of later introduction, but is now much the more common in Italy. It is planted as food for silkworms, and in some parts of Emilia, perhaps also elsewhere, it supports the vine.

Flower, April and May.
Italian name, Moro.

Muscus

MUSCUS.

> 'stagna virentia musco' (*Ge.* iv. 18).
> 'muscosi fontes' (*Ec.* vii. 45).
> 'flumina, muscus ubi et viridissima gramine ripa'
> > (*Ge.* iii. 144).

The name seems to be applied especially to the larger mosses and their kindred, sphagnum and others, which grow in damp ground.

MYRICA.

> 'illum . . . etiam flevere myricae' (*Ec.* x. 13).
> 'te nostrae, Vare, myricae, | te nemus omne canet'
> > (*Ec.* vi. 10).
> 'humiles . . . myricae' (*Ec.* iv. 2).

The tamarisk (Tamarix Gallica) is a familiar object on the Sicilian coasts, and figures as such in Theocritus. From him Virgil must have taken it, for he is not likely to have seen the shrub in his youth, though it is occasionally found by inland marshes. Another species of the genus was sacred to Apollo, and doubtless Virgil alludes to this. Thus he takes it as the emblem of the pastoral poet, coupling it with the vineyards whereof he sings. In *Ec.* viii. 54 the shepherd refers to tamarisks producing amber as a thing that could not be.

In Cornwall the shrub is used for hedges, its slender leaves enabling it to defy the Atlantic gales.

> Flower, April and May.
> Italian names, Tamarice and Brula.

Trees, Shrubs, and Plants of Virgil

MYRTUS.

'Paphiae . . . myrtus' (*Ge.* ii. 64).
'amantes litora myrtus' (*Ge.* iv. 124).

The graceful habit and pleasing scent of the myrtle (Myrtus communis) brought it early into cultivation, and the Hebrew poets made it supplant the thorn and the brier in the new earth. Indeed, though now well established in Italy, it is possibly of Oriental origin. In Theophrastus' time there were already several varieties, and he notes that the one which grew on the Tyrrhene coast was of dwarf habit. This is possibly the Tarentine or small-leaved variety, which is still in cultivation. The tree seldom exceeds twelve feet in height, and Sir Arthur Hort does Theophrastus an injustice in making him say that some myrtles are large trees.

The myrtle is common on south Italian coasts, and between Taranto and Reggio often makes a considerable scrub, though it is sometimes swept away by the spring floods of the fiumicini. Its liking for the shore perhaps accounts for its dedication to Venus, to whose temple at Paphos Virgil's epithet alludes. To compliment Octavian on his supposed descent from Aeneas Virgil makes the world crown his temples 'materna myrto' (*Ge.* i. 28), with the favourite sprays of his divine ancestress. Even in Hades luckless lovers live in a grove of myrtle (*Ae.* vi. 443).

In early days the myrtle, like the cornel, supplied shafts for spears, 'validis hastilibus' (*Ge.* ii. 447), but for this purpose it was supplanted by the ash. When Virgil makes Camilla carry 'pastoralem prae-

Myrtus

fixa cuspide myrtum' (*Ae*. vii. 817) he perhaps implies that as a warrior the Volscian damsel, for all her gallantry, was something of an amateur.

Virgil in his boyhood can have known the myrtle only as a cultivated plant, for the winters of Mantova are too severe for it to grow without protection, and Menalcas has to defend it against the frosts with mats (*Ec*. vii. 6). Even at Rome the two trees in the sanctuary of Quirinus, known as the patrician and the plebeian myrtle, may sometimes have called for like protection. The Sicilian Corydon, who joins it in his nosegay with the bay (*Ec*. ii. 55), could leave it undefended.

The skin of the berry is blackish, but the vinous juice is near enough in colour to blood for an ancient to call the berries 'cruenta' (*Ge*. i. 306). They were gathered in winter and mixed with wine as a remedy for the colic and for toothaches.

Flower, July.
Italian name, Mirto.

NARCISSUS.

> 'sera comantem | narcissum' (*Ge*. iv. 122).
> 'purpurea narcisso' (*Ec*. v. 38).
> 'narcissi lacrimam' (*Ge*. iv. 160).

This name covers several species, and it is probable that the 'purple' narcissus is the pheasant's eye, N. poeticus, or poet's narciss, the epithet having the same sense us in Shelley's 'purple swans.' The tear is that of the youth who was changed into the flower, though in fact the plant has nothing that can be called lacrima. Evidently the word is taken from δάκρυον, which means a bulblet formed in the axles of the leaves as in the tiger-lily. Virgil says that the bees use this tear for the foundation of the combs or, as Mr. Royds interprets it, the propolis by which the comb is glued to the hive. Here the poet cannot have been writing from his own observation, but he returns to it when he adds that the bees also use glue gathered from trees.

The flower of our first passage can be certainly identified through two statements of Theophrastus. He says that the plant blossoms in autumn and that the scape appears before the leaves. The only species which answers to this statement is N. serotinus. It agrees also with the rest of Theophrastus' description. It has a white perianth with a yellowish cup, and it blossoms in September. Virgil's phrase implies that there are vernal species as well.

The plant is not common in Italy, but it is found near Otranto, and the old Corycian may well have got it thence. Virgil does not actually state that his acquaintance grew it, but he seems to imply as much.

> Flower, April and May (N. poeticus); September (N. serotinus).
>
> Italian names, Fior-magga, Narciso, Giracapo, (N. poeticus).

(The autumn narcissus is nowhere common enough to have received a popular name.)

Nasturtium

> 'trahunt acri voltus nasturtia morsu' (*Mor.* 84).

Cress (Lepidium sativum) is an Egyptian plant which came early into cultivation for use in salads. Its name it got from the pungency which twists the nostril. We avoid an excess of pungency by eating the plant in a young state.

> Flower, spring and summer.
> Italian name, Crescione.

NUX.

> 'contemplator item cum nux se plurima silvis
> induet in florem et ramos curvabit olentes' (*Ge.* i. 187).
> 'sparge, marite, nuces' (*Ec.* viii. 31).

It is evident from many passages, and Macrobius expressly tells us that 'nux' as the name of a fruit applied to any that had hard shells. As the name of a tree it stands with a qualifying adjective for several species, but used without an epithet it means the walnut (Juglans regia), still in Italy called *noce*. The Greeks recognized that the tree was of Persian origin, but it must have been early in cultivation, and the Roman name of 'iuglans,' which is 'Iovis glans,' Jove's acorn, like 'Iuniperus,' which is Juno's pear, must have been an early formation.

The flowers of the walnut are unisexual, the male in catkins and the female in clusters. Virgil's 'ramos curvabit' picturesquely describes the drooping catkins. The strong scent which he mentions is said by Pliny to strike into the very brain of who-

Trees, Shrubs, and Plants of Virgil

soever encounters it, and other authorities describe it as poisonous to neighbouring trees. This seems to be a mistake, but of course its thick shade would be bad for an apple or pear growing to the north of it.

Those who think that Virgil's tree is the almond have to face insuperable difficulties. No passage is quoted in which the name without an epithet expressed or implied means anything but the walnut. The almond is 'Nux Graeca' or 'Nux Amygdalina.' Tibullus, speaking of the dyeing of grey hair with walnut juice, says, 'viridi cortice tincta nucis,' and Pliny expressly states that the 'nuces' which the bridegroom threw to the boys for a scramble were walnuts, while the 'nuces' used as children's playthings were admittedly walnut shells. It has been objected that Virgil would not describe the walnut as bending its scented boughs, but he does not, for 'ramos' clearly refers to the catkins. In no case would his words suit the almond, for the almond blossom does not curve the boughs. It is true that the flowers of the walnut are not conspicuous, but they are numerous, and Virgil tells his farmer to examine them for a special purpose.

Flower, April.
Italian name, Noce.

OLEASTER, OR OLEA SILVESTRIS.

'foliis oleaster amaris' (*Ge.* ii. 314 ; *Ae.* xii. 766).

The wild olive (Olea Europaea) is either a native or at least a well-established denizen in southern

Oleaster, or Olea Silvestris

Italy. It has shorter and stiffer leaves than the cultivated variety, and their under-surfaces soon lose the heaviness which in the other is permanent. The berry is small and worthless.

Virgil finds a use for the tree as a shade for a beehive, and as a tree of grazing ground it was sometimes, as in our second passage, consecrated to Faunus, whom the Roman poets identified with Pan. Mr. Fowler, however, views Faunus as essentially a god of the wild.

The oleaster was used as a stock on which to graft the olive. To this practice Virgil objects (*Ge.* ii. 302-314) on the ground that, if there be a fire in the oliveyard, the trees will be burnt below the grafting point, and as the olives are not on their own roots, 'non a stirpe valent,' only the oleaster will remain. Palladius meets this objection by saying that the graft must be made below the surface of the ground, in which case the olive will survive the fire. Our gardeners practise this subterranean grafting with the clematis, the Moutan peony, and other plants.

Unfortunately, in this passage either Virgil was careless in his arrangement or, more probably, there has been some dislocation in his text. The lines, as they stand in the manuscripts, come in the middle of his account of the vine. Hence some editors have supposed him to mean that oleasters should not be planted in a vineyard. This interpretation agrees neither with the Latin, for 'insere' must mean graft, nor with reason, for the fire would be equally fatal to the olives whether they were planted among vines or not. It is clear that Palladius understood the passage in the only possible sense.

The crook on which the shepherd leans (*Ec.* viii. 16) is of the wild olive, for the word in Theocritus, whom Virgil followed, is ἀγριελαίω. It may well be doubted whether, when the poem was written, Virgil had yet seen an olive. There cannot have been any near Mantova.

> Flower, July and August.
> Italian name, Oleastro.

OLIVA, OR OLEA.

> 'pingues ... olivae' (*Ge.* ii. 85).
> 'pallenti ... olivae' (*Ec.* v. 16).

Of all Italian trees the olive (Olea sativa) was naturally held of most account, and could be called 'the tree' without qualification, as in Horace's 'arbore nunc aquas culpante.' It is a cultivated variety of O. Europaea, which perhaps has no native claim to its specific designation. Its Latin names probably came from the Greek ἐλαία, the form 'oliva' from a dialect in which the digamma was still spoken, and 'olea' from one from which the digamma had disappeared. This seems to point to a somewhat late introduction into Italy, and it may have been brought by the earliest Greek colonists. The tree is too tender to grow at high altitudes or, except on warm coastlands, in the north of Italy, and the parts in which it flourishes are known as the region of the olive.

Oliva, or Olea

The lanceolate and pointed leaves at once distinguish our tree from the oleaster, and the heaviness of the under-surface does not disappear with age as it does in the wild form. The panicles of small white blossoms appear in August. The green fruit ripens into black, and the first gathering is late in November. There was, however, one variety which was gathered unripe to provide green oil for salads. It was harvested in September.

In Italy the tree broke into varieties, of which Virgil selects three for his verse (*Ge.* ii. 86). Cato names ten and Columella ten or possibly eleven, each list including Virgil's three. The kind called 'orchites,' which Virgil for the convenience of his verse calls 'orchades,' bears a title like that which Queen Gertrude's liberal shepherds gave to the long purples, and in shape it must have resembled the tuber of an orchid. On its qualities Pliny and Columella are at issue, the one holding that it gave abundant oil and the other that it was fit only for eating. Martyn seems to err in identifying it with the modern 'olivola,' which is small and round. The kind called 'radius,' from its resemblance to a weaver's shuttle, is still known as 'raggaria,' an oblong olive, producing a very sweet oil, but in small quantities. The third kind was called 'pausia,' or in the popular speech 'posea,' a name of which the derivation does not appear. This was the kind that gave the green oil. Virgil does not mention the kind called 'Sergia,' which produced the largest amount of oil. It was named after a member of the house

Trees, Shrubs, and Plants of Virgil

of Sergius, and is one of the sixteen varieties named by Macrobius.

Two methods of propagation mentioned by Virgil are still in vogue. One (*Ge.* ii. 63) is much like what Shirley Hibberd calls the currant-tree method of propagating roses. A small branch, not more than two inches in diameter at its thickest point, is sawn off the tree, care being taken not to jag the bark. The lower part of this branch is cut into lengths of a foot or a foot and a half. These cuttings or truncheons, 'trunci' or 'taleae,' are then pointed at both ends and buried nearly their whole length in the nursery. It takes five years before they can be transplanted to their places in the oliveyard. Sometimes they are not set in the nursery for transplantation, but set in the yard at once. In this case they were cut to the length of three feet.

The second method (*ib.* 30) has the advantage that the transplanting can be done after three years, but the trees were thought to be not so good. The trunk of an old tree is cut into small pieces with a strip of bark at one side. These are planted like the truncheons and soon produce roots. The mulberry shares with the olive this power of producing roots from old wood. Pliny tells stories, not, as some of his stories are, impossible, of olive wood sprouting even after it had passed through the carpenter's hands.

With grafting I have dealt in the previous article.

Virgil tells us that when olive-trees are once established they need no more cultivation (*ib.* 420), but

Oliva, or Olea

this must not be taken quite literally. In his day, as now, the ground under the branches was dug every year, every few years manure was applied, and every eighth year some pruning was done. Virgil means that all this was nothing to the many labours of the vineyard.

Concerning the use of olives and oil for food, for cookery, for an unguent, and for artificial light, there are a few touches in the poems. There is the oil lamp that sputters as a sign of coming rain (*Ge.* i. 393); there is the slippery oil with which above the cliffs of Actium the Trojan athletes anointed themselves to celebrate their escape from their Greek foes (*Ae.* iii. 281); and there is the fling at the town exquisite who spoils his unguent with perfumes (*Ge.* ii. 466). The victors in the games are crowned with olive blossoms, which drop upon their yellow pollen (*Ae.* v. 309). The victim on the altar burns the quicker for the oil that is poured over it (*Ae.* vi. 254). Nor does the use of oil cease with a man's life. Together with frankincense and food it has its place on the funeral pyre (*ib.* 225).

Just as in Bentley's phrase the very dust of Pearson's writings is gold, so the watery part of the olive (amurca) was valuable for steeping seeds (*Ge.* i. 194), for use in a sheep dip (*Ge.* iii. 448), and for other purposes.

In face of all these uses it seems strange that for a farm of sixty acres Cato gives the olive only the fourth place. First comes the vineyard and then the irrigated garden and the willow bed.

Trees, Shrubs, and Plants of Virgil

It might be thought that the trees were too precious to be cut as timber, but Theophrastus mentions some uses of it, one of them the fuel for a furnace. Possibly, like the shepherd's staff, this was the wood of the oleaster. It may be surmised that the same explanation will hold of 'viridi' as applied to the wreath given to Mnestheus, as it seems, for being second in the boat race (*Ae*. v. 493), the winner's wreath being of bay. Virgil would hardly apply the epithet to a wreath of the grey olive, unless indeed he means that the spray had a few green berries on it. Horace's allusion in 'viridi Venafro' is to the berry, not, as some editors suppose, to the leaves.

There was yet another part played by the olive in a world too well acquainted with war. The Romans adopted the legend that Athena was the inventor of the olive (*Ge*. i. 18), but it hardly needed this association with the queen of arts and crafts to make the rich olive the emblem of peace. It is the envoy's white flag (*Ae*. vii. 154, 751, viii. 116), and Aeneas in the vain hope of a peaceful reception in Italy crowns himself with olive leaves when on leaving Sicily for the second time he makes his offering of wine and entrails to the powers of the sea (*Ae*. v. 774).

Flower, July and August.
Italian names, Olivo and Ulivo.

Ornus

ORNUS.

'nascuntur steriles saxosis montibus orni' (*Ge.* ii. 111).

Columella says that this tree is a wild ash with broader leaves. It is the manna ash (Fraxinus ornus), which is with some reason regarded by the Latin poets as the typical hillside tree of central and southern Italy. Handsome and free flowering, it is of much less stature than its cousin tree. Virgil makes Linus say that Hesiod's pipe would draw the manna ashes down from the mountains (*Ec.* vi. 71).

The wood is said to be pliant, and Theophrastus says it was employed for elastic bedsteads, for some carpenter's tools, and, it would seem, for the curved parts of merchant ships. Virgil happens to mention it several times together with other timbers in connection with funeral pyres, but it may be supposed that for this purpose men took what they could get.

The tree is not much planted in England, but grafted on the common ash it will flourish even in large towns.

The supposition that Ornus was the rowan is quite groundless.

Flower, May.
Italian name, Orniello.

PALIURUS.

'spinis surgit paliurus acutis' (*Ec.* v. 39).

The death of Daphnis, which apart from allegory is the murder of Caesar, is supposed by Virgil to give to the noxious wildings a mastery over the flowers worthy of a garden. Few plants are more masterful in occupying land than what is known as Christ's thorn (Paliurus aculeatus). The plant is common in Palestine, and disputes with *Zizyphus Spina Christi* the claim to have supplied the crown of thorns at the Crucifixion. Its so-called thorns are in fact stipular prickles. In the decay of Etruria the plant went ahead to such an extent that in warfare it could play the part now assigned to barbed wire, for it is probably the shrub through whose thickets Polybius tells us the Gauls could not pass to attack the Romans until they had stripped off their clothes (ii. 28). Dennis, who refers to this passage, was himself kept away by the shrub from the walls of Rusellae, but had not the curiosity to learn its botanical name. 'The area of the city and the slopes around it are densely covered with a thorny shrub called "marruca," which I had often admired elsewhere for its bright yellow blossoms and delicate foliage; but as an antagonist it is most formidable, particularly in winter, when its fierceness is unmitigated by a leafy covering. Even could one disregard the thorns, the difficulty of forcing one's way through the thickets is so great that some of the finest portions of the walls are unapproachable from below.' It will be seen that Columella had reason in recommending the shrub for hedges.

The natural order to which 'marruca' belongs is represented in England by the two buckthorns, one of which has formidable spines, and in America is

Paliurus

planted for hedges. The vine also is a kindred
plant, but has always preferred vengeance to self-
defence.

> Flower, May and June.
> Italian name, Marruca.

PALMA.

> ' mittit . . . Eliadum palmas Epiros equarum' (*Ge.* i. 59).
> ' ardua palma ' (*Ge.* ii. 67).
> ' primus Idumaeas referam tibi Mantua palmas ' (*Ge.* iii. 12).

Although there are many genera and species of
palms, one of which, Chamaerops humilis, is a
native of Sicily, Virgil refers only to the date palm,
Phoenix dactylifera. The epithet of ' ardua,' which
Virgil applies to it, must refer to the great length of
the stem, at the top of which is the foliage and the
fruit. It must have been imported at an early date
into Sicily and southern Italy. In Virgil's days,
although Selinunte, ' palmosa Selinus' (*Ae.* iii. 705),
was already a ruined city, there must have been
palms planted along its sea front, as there still are
some thirty miles off at Trapani. At both places
you may find Chamaerops, on the sides of the Eryx
in great abundance, but only as a stunted shrub.

In Arabia and parts of Africa the date was much
used for food, while in Palestine, Greece, and Italy
the leaves were early regarded as a symbol of peace
and victory. Virgil's reference to the palms˙ of
Edom is allegorical and difficult. His probable
meaning is that he hopes some day to celebrate
the victories of Octavian and the pacification of the

world. When the time came for him to do this he shrank from the task, and, although he accomplished it in the Aeneid, he avowed that he must have been mad to undertake it.

Flower, summer.
Italian name, Palma da datteri.

PANACEA.

'odoriferam panaceam' (*Ae*. xii. 419).

The plant here is clearly mythical, though there is a Greek plant of the name which has been identified with a near relative of the parsnip. These plants are of a sugary and scented tribe, and panacea cannot be answerable for its kinswort. Still it is better to keep the parsnip, like the hatter, at a distance from epic poetry. It shall therefore be judged that Virgil's plant is not that of Theophrastus, but a child of his own fancy. There are no fields of all-heal 'on this side of the grave.'

PAPAVER.

'campum . . . urunt Lethaeo perfusa papavera somno'
(*Ge*. i. 78).

'Cereale papaver' (*Ib*. 212).
umida mella soporiferumque papaver' (*Ae*. iv. 486).
'summa papavera carpens' (*Ec*. ii. 47).

Although there are six species of poppy native to Italy, Virgil probably deals only with the opium poppy (Papaver somniferum) and its varieties. Pliny speaks of three kinds, the white, the black, and the erratic, which, he says, the Greeks call 'rhoeas.' The last seems to be the round prickly-headed poppy of our chalk fields, while his black poppy is our common scarlet poppy, with the globose and smooth seed vessel.

Of the opium poppy there are two varieties still cultivated in Italy, but in ancient days, while both were grown for their seeds, perhaps only one was grown for opium. It is not clear whether it was grown for this end in Italy, for the drug seems generally to have been imported. This kind, known as P. officinale, has an ovoid capsule and white seeds. It is not, I think, common in our gardens. The other variety, P. hortense, has a globular capsule and black—or at least dark—seeds. This kind is common in our gardens, and has established itself about Cobham and elsewhere in Kent. In a wild state both varieties have white petals slightly tinged with lilac, and carrying a purple blotch at the base. Under cultivation the flowers often are red or crimson on pure white and frequently double.

Our plant is probably a native of Mediterranean Europe and spread eastward with unhappy results. The capsules abound in opium or hashish, which is obtained through incisions made in them as they ripen, the juice coagulating in the night. The seeds, for which the Romans grew the plant, have no narcotic properties, and their oil could be a substitute for the juice of the olive. Unground they were used like our caraway seeds in cakes. This may be one reason for our poet's epithet of 'Cereale,' but no doubt he was thinking also of the frequent repre-

H

sentation of poppies in the statues of Ceres. The current explanation was that she ate the seeds to console herself for the loss of Proserpine. A more plausible account would be that she had recourse to hashish. A more important use of the seeds was their conjunction with honey as the normal sweetener in days when there was no sugar cane or sugar beet.

The meaning of 'vescum' was at one time disputed, but Munro proved that it must mean small. The reference is to the size of the seeds. We should not apply an epithet in this way, but the vetch seems to be called 'tenuis' by Virgil for the same reason.

In our fourth passage Virgil has fallen into one of those confusions to which we are all at times liable. He doubtless meant that the priestess of the Hesperides fed her watch-dragon with cakes of honey and poppy seeds. The seeds, as we have seen, are not soporific; but Virgil was so much in the habit of thinking of the drowsy poppy that in this passage he transfers the epithet from the capsules to the seeds, and makes his priestess put her watch-dragon to sleep. In the same way Horace puts into Juno's mouth the phrase 'quietis ordinibus deorum' at the very moment when she is emphasizing a restlessness in herself which has lasted for centuries. A like inattention was that of the modern nobleman, who said, 'If we cannot move the Church we must appeal to the Dissenters: "flectere si nequeo superos, Acheronta movebo."'

Flower, April and May.
Italian name, Papavero.

Phaselus

PHASELUS.

'vilem . . . phaselum' (*Ge.* i. 227).

English editors of Virgil have gone much astray on this plant, most of them identifying it with the kidney bean or scarlet runner. Even if they did not know that these plants are American, they should have been warned by Virgil's advice to sow the plant in November, for the kidney bean will bear no touch of frost, and we do not sow it in the open until May. Virgil's plant is Dolichus melanophthalmus, an Asiatic, still common in Italian eating-houses under the name of ' fagiolo dall' occhio,' the eye bean. The ancients ate the whole pod as we do French beans. Virgil's epithet is perhaps unduly derogatory to a useful vegetable.

The boat called ' phaselus ' is supposed to have got its name from a resemblance to the fagiolo dall' occhio.

Flower, summer.

Italian name. See above.

PICEA.

'nigranti picea' (*Ae.* ix. 87).
' Naryciae . . . picis lucos' (*Ge.* ii. 438).
' Idaeas . . . pices' (*Ge.* iii. 450).

Although the identification of this tree has been disputed, there are truths which seem to point to a definite conclusion. It was the tree which produced the best pitch, and the best pitch came from the mountains of the extreme south. The tree of those mountains is the Corsican pine (Pinus Laricio), easily distinguished, as Veitch says, 'by its strict, erect habit, by its shortened branches, which sometimes show a tendency to curve in a direction round the tree and upwards, and by its large, twisted, glaucous foliage.'

Naryx is a town of the Opuntian Locri in Greece, of which people the Italian city of Locri was held to be a colony, and it is to the Italian city that Virgil refers. It lies under the great range of Sila, which he makes the scene of the fight of bulls (*Ae.* xii. 715, sqq.). Doubtless pitch was largely exported from Locri to other parts of Italy. Farmers did not usually make their own pitch, few of them having trees at hand, but bought it in the market towns and melted it into tar (*Ge.* i. 225). It was used, as with us, for a preservative of timber, for an ingredient in a sheep-wash (*Ge.* iii. 450), and for marking corn-sacks (*Ge.* ii. 263). It was also smeared on the corks of wine-jars, as we put wax on the corks of bottles. Nowadays in the Apennines the wine that is kept for domestic use is often put into bottles. These stand upright, and, instead of corks and tar, a few drops of oil are put on the top. When the wine is to be drunk the oil is sucked up by means of a little cotton-wool.

The tree was well fitted to make a funeral pyre, but when in our first passage Virgil makes Aeneas employ it for the cremation of Misenus he must have forgotten that the tree did not grow near the sea-level.

Picea

The trunk of this pine was largely used for sub-terranean water-pipes, as under the ground it did not decay. For pipes above ground other material had to be employed.

Flower, February and March.
Italian name, Pino di Corsica.

PINUS.

'pulcherrima pinus in hortis' (*Ec.* vii. 65).
'nautica pinus' (*Ec.* iv. 38).

It is clear that at least two species are included under this generic name. One is a tree of the south and the lowlands, the other of the north and the hills. The first is the stone or parasol pine (Pinus pinea), a familiar object in the scenery of central and southern Italy, but not coming much north of the famous forest which it makes near Ravenna. This is the tree of our first passage. The other is our own Scotch fir (P. silvestris), which is chiefly an Alpine, but occurs in the Genoese Apennines, and as far south as the Parmesan district. This must be the tree of the Vesulan woods which concealed the wild boar (*A e.* x. 708), and also that which the bee-keeper is enjoined to bring from the high hills (*Ge.* iv. 112). The stone pine is easily recognized by its habit and large round cones.

Pines were sacred to Cybele, Attis, and Pan or Faunus. Pan's home was Mount Maenalus in Arcadia, which always has 'argutumque nemus pinosque loquentes' (*Ec.* viii. 22). The trees make their own music in the wind and also echo the notes of Pan and the Shepherds. Sir James Frazer suggests that one reason for the association of the pine with Attis may have been the value of its seeds as food. They are still gathered in Italy and sold and eaten as fruit.

Pine wood was used not only for shipbuilding but also for fuel. Sprays of the trees were used for skimming pots of must or fermenting grape juice (*Ge.* i. 296). Virgil's word for the spray is 'folium,' and Pliny tells us that this word meant a spray of a coniferous tree.

It should be added that the dominant pine on Mount Ida appears to be neither of Virgil's species, but one which is found in some sea-coast districts of southern Italy. This is the Aleppo pine (P. Haleponsis), which, according to Theophrastus, was the chief shipbuilding tree of Cyprus. It is probably included under Virgil's name. It is a slender tree, not growing to a great height.

> Flower, February to April.
> Italian names: Pino da pinocchi (Stone pine).
>   Pino di Scozia (Scotch fir).

PIRUS.

> 'insere nunc, Meliboee, piros' (*Ec.* i. 13 ; cf. *Ec.* ix. 50).
> 'ornus . . . incanuit albo | flore piri' (*Ge.* ii. 71).
> 'in versum distulit . . . eduram . . . pirum' (*Ge.* iv. 144).

Virgil's pear seems to be Pyrus domestica, which may or may not be a cultivated form of the wild pear (P. communis). It had already developed into several varieties, of which Virgil mentions the Syrian,

Pirus

the Crustumine, and the Volemum (*Ge.* ii. 88). According to Pliny and Columella the second was the best, but none were accounted very wholesome unless stewed in wine. The Syrian, called also the Tarentine, may be the bergamot. The third kind is said to get its name from 'vola,' the palm of the hand, which one fruit would fill, and is perhaps the same as Pliny's 'librale' or pound pear. Martial mentions a good kind, which 'docta Neapolis creavit,' and Naples retains its renown for good horticulture.

The pear-tree was used, as it still is, for a stock on which to graft apples (*Ge.* ii. 33). Virgil held that the pear itself could be grafted on the manna ash, but there is no kinship between the two.

The wild pear sometimes makes large woods, as on some of the lower slopes of Soracte, which in spring are white with its blossom.

Flower, April and May.
Italian name, Pero.

PLATANUS.

'platani steriles' (*Ge.* ii. 70).

The plane (Platanus Orientalis), as a native tree, does not come west of Greece, though Theophrastus held that it was native to one Adriatic island. Pliny, however, says that it was planted there. It was, however, extensively planted and has established itself along the rivers and the fiumicini of Calabria. It seems to have taken a long time to become acclimatized, for the same Greek authority says that the trees planted at Reggio by Dionysius never attained any size. One would, however, gather that in Augustan times it was a fine tree in much more northerly situations. In our days there are magnificent trees at Bologna.

It seems to owe its name to its broad leaves (πλατύς), and it was planted only for its beauty and for shade. Its habit of shaling its bark made it unfit to support the vine, and it was hence called ' caelebs,' the bachelor tree. It also seems doubtful whether it would survive the treatment which the elm and the willow underwent when they were used in the vineyard. The size of its leaves is sometimes assigned as a reason, but this would hardly count if it were reduced to a single shoot.

It was customary in summer to hold the symposium under its shade, and the old Corycian was able to transplant it when it was already large enough for this end, 'ministrantem platanum potantibus umbras' (Ge. iv. 146).

The London plane is a variety which seems to have been developed in the great city itself. Its liking for a city life used to be ascribed to the shaling of its bark, but it is now recognized that London dirt does its harm not through the bark, but through the buds and leaves, in which point the plane is no better off than its fellows. Its fruit, which breaks up in the spring, has come under some suspicion as a contributory cause of catarrh. It had this reputation with Dioscorides, and London newspapers have

Platanus

lately admitted correspondence on the subject. The guilt of the tree seems to be unproved.

The inhabitants of Cos show a tree whose trunk has a diameter of six yards, and they profess to believe that it is old enough for Hippocrates to have sat under it.

Flower, April and May.

Italian name, Platano.

POPULUS.

> ' candida populus ' (*Ec.* ix. 41).
> ' bicolor . . . populus ' (*Ae.* viii. 276).
> ' populus in silvis pulcherrima ' (*Ec.* vii. 65).
> ' populus Alcidae gratissima ' (*Ib.* 61).

Whether the abele or white poplar (Populus alba) be a native or an importation from eastern Europe, it was at any rate well established along the watercourses and in the wet woods of Italy. The young shoots are very white and cottony, and the leaves are green above and white beneath. The tree is sometimes nearly a hundred feet high. Its wood is useful wherever lightness and whiteness are desired.

Hercules, on his return from the lower world, made himself a chaplet of poplar leaves, and Homer's name of ἀχέρωις marks the tree as a denizen of Hades.

Both the black poplar and the aspen must have been known to Virgil, but he makes no direct mention of either. It is from the former that bees get much 'fucus,' the rosinous substance used for propolis (*Ge.* iv. 39).

Trees, Shrubs, and Plants of Virgil

The white poplar is not a native of England, and does not often make a good tree in this country. In popular parlance its name is often transferred to the grey poplar (P. canescens), which is a native both here and in northern Italy. It may be distinguished by the colour and by the toothed and angled leaves of the suckers. Virgil's eye must have seen the difference between these two trees.

Where the climate was too hot for the oak, as at Olympia, the abele took its place as a coronary plant.

Flower, March and April.
Italian names, Alberello and Gattice.

PORRUM (*Porrum capitatum*).

' capiti nomen debentia porri' (*Mor.* 74).

The leek (Allium porrum) is an Oriental plant, which very early came into cultivation. Except for an increase of size, it seems to have changed little since Roman times. Columella says that the best were grown at Ariccia at the foot of the Alban hills, a town famous for other vegetables as well.

The other Roman porrum, called 'sectile,' was chives (A. schoenoprasum), is also common in our gardens, and is interesting to us by reason of its two isolated stations in this country, one in Cornwall, the other along a basaltic dyke in Northumberland. It has no Continental station in western Europe.

Flower, June and July.
Italian names: Porro (leek).
Cipolline (chives).

Prunus and Spinus

'cerea pruna' (*Ec.* ii. 53).
'spinos iam pruna ferentes' (*Ge.* iv. 145).

The plum (Prunus communis) is divided into several sub-species, and of these one at least had broken into so many varieties that Pliny could say, 'ingens turba prunorum.' This is P. domestica, of which the wild fruit is very dark. In cultivation the blue plums were less valued than the yellow or, as Virgil calls them, the waxen, such as our golden drop.

Virgil's 'spinus' is the blackthorn or sloe, under whose thickets the Sicilian lizards take refuge from the midday heat (*Ec.* ii. 9). It was used as a stock for grafting the plum, while the wild plum itself and the bullace (P. insititia) were used as stocks for the cornel (*Ge.* ii. 34). The blackthorn is a common hedge shrub in Italy, but the wild plum seems to be found only in cultivation. It should be said that Arcangeli's P. communis is the almond. His name for the plum, which he makes a distinct species, is P. domestica.

Flower, March and April.
Italian names: Susino (plum).
Prugnolo and Vegro (sloe).

ROBUR, QUERCUS, AESCULUS.

The two forms of the English oak are so closely allied that modern botanists refuse them specific rank, and class them as varieties. The botanical

differences are that in Quercus pedunculata, the
common oak, the leaves have no stalk, while the
acorn has a long one; whereas in Q. sessiliflora, the
durmast oak, the characters are reversed, the leaf
having a stalk, and the acorn so short a one as
hardly to count. The gardener distinguishes the
latter as having a straighter and more regular stem
and larger and more numerous leaves. Experiments
seem to show that the durmast oak can boast the
tougher timber, and an old belief that it was less
lasting seems to have no foundation.

Small as the differences may be, Virgil clearly distinguished the two varieties—

'Nemorumque Iovi quae maxima frondet
Aesculus, atque habitae Graiis oracula quercus'
(*Ge.* ii. 15).

The difference of size, upon which he here fixes,
probably refers to the appearance of the trees in leaf,
for it seems that in the diameter of the trunk and
the dimensions of the limbs neither tree has any
advantage over the other. It is the density of leafage
that magnifies the bulk of the durmast. Nor is this
all, for its leaves are less liable to disease and to the
ravages of caterpillars, frequent causes of disfigure-
ment to its less fortunate congener. On the other
hand, the comparative uprightness of its branches
detracts somewhat from its dignity.

The favourite habitats of the two varieties differ
in Italy as they do in England. The durmast, as
Mr. Robinson tells us, inhabits plateaux and slopes
of hills and mountains, while the common oak is

best in heavy soils and lower ground. Arcangeli makes a like remark concerning their habits in Italy. Nor in Italy are the two varieties, as with us, geographically interspersed. The durmast is rare in the north and the common oak hardly to be found in the south.

Just as we use the name of oak indiscriminately of either variety, so Virgil and the Latins generally use the name of 'quercus' and the Italians the name of 'querce.' When a distinction is made the modern usage differs from Virgil's, the name of 'eschio' (aesculus) being applied to the common oak, while the durmast is known as 'rovere' (robur).

The striking of an oak by lightning was of course accounted an omen (*Ec.* i. 17), and in fact makes a wonderful sight. Some years since a very fine but quite sound oak in Tewkesbury Park was so struck, and only about six feet of the huge trunk left standing. Round the tree a circle with a diameter of a hundred yards was covered with branches great and small, a blow from which might well have killed a man if he had been within the range. The peasantry avowed that timber so struck would not make fuel, but this was easily disproved.

The bier, feretrum, on which a dead body was laid for burning, was made of cypress and oak (*Ae.* xi. 65).

It should be added that Pliny uses robur as the name of a distinct species. This is the Turkey oak, Q. cerris, whose acorn, as he rightly says, is bitter and rough, and bristly like a chestnut. The Romans held that the shingles which roofed the houses of early Rome were made of this tree.

> Flower, April and May.
> Italian names: Eschio and Farnia (Quercus
> pedunculata).
> Rovere (Q. sessiliflora).
> Cerro (Q. cerris).

Ros, or Ros Marinus (*Ge.* ii. 213).

The rosemary (Rosmarinus officinalis) gets its name from its liking for sea coasts and spray. In the inland parts of Italy it is found only in cultivation. Virgil speaks of it as a bee plant on thin gravel soils, and implies that it will hardly grow on them. There is, however, no difficulty in cultivating it, and in this country it was once in high repute. It was grown for its scent and for the tonic oil supplied by its tops, and accounted a cure for headaches. Its long flowering season may make it useful for the yield of honey.

There seems to be no ancient authority for its association with remembrance, but Ophelia's phrase was an old one in England.

> Flower, March to October.
> Italian names, Ramerino and Rosmarino.

Rosa

ROSA.

'puniceis . . . rosetis' (*Ec.* v. 17).
'mixta rubent ubi lilia multa | alba rosa' (*Ae.* xii. 69).
'biferi . . . rosaria Paesti' (*Ge.* iv. 119).

Virgil was probably acquainted with three exotic and several native species of the rose, and the foreigners had already broken into varieties and produced double or at least semi-double flowers.

The cabbage or Provence rose (Rosa centifolia) has a specific name, which Linnaeus took from Pliny, and which refers to the double flower, which is a product of cultivation. Mr. Pemberton calls this rose a native of the south of France, but this statement seems to be without warrant, and the higher authority of Nicholson is doubtless right in assigning to it an Asiatic home. Travellers still find it in the Caucasas, from whence it came to Greece. In Greece it is said to have naturalized itself, but not so in Italy. Theophrastus knew the flower in its single state, for he says that it has a flower within a flower, the inner being in fact the stamens and pistils. He compares its colour with the oleander and the rosy petal-tips of the so-called Egyptian bean of Pythagoras. It may be distinguished from the damask rose by its spreading sepals and less rigid leaves. From it descend our cabbage and moss roses.

Of the damask rose (R. Damascena) Mr. Pemberton remarks that it was first brought to the notice of Europeans by the Crusaders, but there seems no reason to doubt that it was known to the Romans. It may be Pliny's Milesian rose, which he describes as having the brightest colours, but not more than twelve petals. The gardeners of Miletus probably imported it from Damascus, where Kinglake in *Eothen* speaks of it as growing to an immense height. Some of its varieties are extremely vigorous in this country. I have a specimen of the kind called Lady Curzon, some ten years old, which is fifteen feet through and still spreading.

This must be the rose of our third passage, for none other known to the Romans could in any way be said to bloom twice. Of its descendants the Red Monthly and the White Monthly. Mr. Pemberton says that both produce 'a second and even a third crop of flowers in favourable seasons.' Some commentators speak of an autumnal crop of roses at Pesto, but this crop is of their own invention. No ancient authority knows anything of autumnal roses, and the interval between the two crops of the damask is very brief. Considering how short the normal time of blossoming is, we need not wonder that the Romans, who valued the flower so highly, welcomed any lengthening of its season. By Domitian's time they had learnt the art of hastening the flowering season by growing their roses in greenhouses or frames, 'specularia,' which had already been used to give Tiberius cucumbers all the year round. There is, however, no mention of these devices in Virgil's time. The so-called greenhouse of Maecenas on the Esquiline, even if it did contain plants, a thing by no means certain, was, as any gardener can see, in no sense a forcing house.

Virgil's third rose (R. Gallica) claims, though not undisputedly, to be a native of Italy, and is recognized as such by Arcangeli. Its name of the Provins rose comes from the town near Paris where it was cultivated for the manufacture of conserves. Whatever its origin, it has got a strong footing in Europe, and spreads so fast by suckers as to become in some cases a pestilent weed. It is the rose of Assisi, where it fills the garden at Porziuncula, and the red fungus which sometimes stains its leaves has given rise to the fantastic legend that it displays the blood of St. Francis. It has no large prickles, and one could roll in it with little damage. Those who desire torture may get it better from the damask. The best-known representative of the Provins rose in our gardens is the double red and white Rosa Mundi.

Of these roses Pliny and others mention a good many varieties, but it seems impossible to identify them, or to be sure that they remain in cultivation.

To come to native roses, we cannot suppose that Virgil failed to observe the white and fragrant blossoms of R. sempervirens, a hedge plant in all the lower grounds of Italy. We know it best in the double form called Félicité et Perpétué. To this our list must add at least the dog rose and the Scotch brier.

Of the uses of the rose Virgil says no more than that the dried petals make a medicine for sick bees

Trees, Shrubs, and Plants of Virgil

(*Ge.* ii. 466). From poets of a more festive spirit
and stronger constitutions we learn that roses were
worn on the head at dinner and scattered about the
floor, or dropped, as in Nero's golden house, from
a reversible ceiling. The luxurious would lie on the
petals, and the Sybarite complain when these were
laid edgeways. If a Roman died in the flowering
season they were strewn upon his tomb.

Columella's recipe for forcing roses may tempt
some adventurous spirit. At a little distance from
the stem you make a circular, shallow trench as soon
as the flower-buds show, and occasionally fill it with
warm water. It may be presumed that the tempera-
ture must be less than that which proved fatal to the
plantings of Triptolemus Yellowlees.

> Flower, May.
> Italian name, Rosa.

RUBUS.

'rubus asper' (*Ec.* iii. 89).
'rubos horrentes' (*Ge.* iii. 315).
'nunc facilis rubea texatur fiscina virga' (*Ge.* i. 266).

In the brambles or blackberries we have a confusing genus, and of the species Rubus fruticosus
Baker recognized more than thirty varieties in this
country. Arcangeli contents himself with seven
types and a few varieties, and probably Virgil, like
many Englishmen, called them all simply blackberries. As with us, the commonest kind seems to
be R. discolor, which has large pink flowers, white
under-surface to its leaves, and a juicy fruit.

Rubus

Pliny tells us that the withies of the bramble with the prickles removed were used to make baskets. Nevertheless, in our third passage some may prefer to follow Servius in reading *Rubea*, and see a reference to willows, but there is no other evidence that the town of Rubi was famous for willows.

Blackberries, from their likeness to mulberries, were called *mora*, a name surviving in the French ' mûrs sauvages ' and the Italian ' more del rovo ' and ' more di macchia.'

> Flower, June and July.
> Italian names, Rogo and Rovo.

RUMEX.

' fecundus . . . rumex' (*Mor.* 73).

There are many species of dock, but there can be little doubt that ours is the curled dock (Rumex crispus), which still bears the names of ' romice ' and ' rombice.' It is marked by its waved leaves and its growth in dry places, many of the genus having aquatic habits. The name may also cover the fiddle dock (R. pulcher), which owes its name to the shape of the leaves. In Italy it is the most common kind, but in England is not found north of the Midland counties.

The epithet refers to the patience which the plant shows on the gathering of its leaves. They grow again with great rapidity, and no plant seems to suffer less from this treatment. They were cooked and eaten like spinach.

> Flower, May and June.
> Italian names. See above.

RUSCUS.

> 'horridior rusco' (*Ec.* vii. 42).
> 'aspera rusci | vimina' (*Ge.* ii. 413).

The butcher's broom (Ruscus aculeatus) is occasionally wild in southern England, and large patches of it may often be seen on the hills above the Italian lakes. Its flowers and red berries, like those of asparagus, grow on branches which have taken the shape of leaves. Though it dies down every year, its growth is shrubby, and the sharp spines explain Virgil's epithets. In Italy it is still used for making brooms. It can hardly have made good withies for tying up vines, though Virgil seems to imply that it was used for this purpose.

> Flower, February.
> Italian name, Pungi-topo.

RUTA.

> 'rutam . . . rigentem' (*Mor.* 89).

Rue, or the herb of grace (Ruta graveolens), is not a common plant in any part of Italy. It was, however, cultivated, and seems to have played the part which parsley plays with us. Thus it was used to flavour soups and other dishes, and to garnish eggs and the like. As an eye-salve it already had the renown of which we hear in a medieval line,

'Auxilio rutae, vir lippe, videbis acute,'

and in Milton's

'. . . purg'd with Euphrasie and Rue
The visual nerve.'

The name of 'herb of grace' is not ancient, and was perhaps due to a false etymology.

Flower, July and August.
Italian name, Ruta.

SALIUNCA.

'puniceis humilis quantum saliunca rosetis . . . cedit'
(*Ec.* v. 17).

The Celtic nard (Valeriana Celtica), though found in the Piedmontese Alps, was not a native of Italy in the more ancient sense. It was, however, cultivated for use in perfumery, as was at one time our own wild valerian. The flowers are usually yellowish, but it is said that they are sometimes red, and to this colour Virgil refers. Its scent also was like that of the rose. Keightley supposed Virgil to allude to the use of roses in chaplets, for which the valerian would be too brittle. I see no such allusion. The poet seems to be talking of garden beds.

Flower, July.

Trees, Shrubs, and Plants of Virgil

SALIX AND SILER.

'genus haud unum . . . salici' (*Ge.* ii. 83).
'viminibus salices fecundae' (*ib.* 446).
'dulce . . . lenta salix feto pecori' (*Ec.* iii. 83).
'(apes) pascuntur . . . glaucas salices' (*Ge.* iv. 182).
'lenta salix . . . pallenti cedit olivae' (*Ec.* v. 16).
'vescas salicum frondes' (*Ge.* iii. 175).
'glauca canentia fronde salicta' (*Ge.* ii. 13).
'salignas . . . umbonum crates' (*Ae.* vii. 632).
'molle siler' (*Ge.* ii. 12).

The willow tribe are a large and confusing people, and, since modern botanists are at issue concerning them, we cannot expect Virgil to be exact in his specific distinctions. He, of course, recognized that there were several species (*Ge.* ii. 84). Arcangeli counts twenty-seven in Italy beside varieties and hybrids. Some of these, however, are not native, the osier (Salix viminalis) being one. This is of northern origin, was not known to the ancient Romans, and even now is not much cultivated south of Lombardy. Linnaeus was less happy than usual in his specific name, for, while Juvenal may well be right in calling the viminal 'dictum a vimine collem,' this must have been another species, probably the purple osier (S. purpurea), of which there may have been a bed at the foot of the hill. This was probably the Amerine willow (*Ge.* i. 265), which supplied withies for tying vines. It grows to some nine feet high, and is common on some of our English streams. Columella speaks of its red stems.

Round Mantova willows, especially S. triandra,

were and are used to support the vines, and amid these Gallus desired to lie:

'mecum inter salices lenta sub vite iaceret' (*Ec.* x. 40).

The willow which Menalcas avows to be less beautiful than the olive was probably the white willow (S. alba), which, however, greatly exceeds the olive in stature and, as some may think, in beauty.

Goats feed on the leaves of various willows and bees go to the flowers for honey. Virgil knew them as hedge plants (*Ge.* ii. 434). Shields in old days had been made of wicker-work, and the wood made the sickle of Priapus (*Ge.* iv. 110). Virgil's references to ties and withies are numerous, and our nurserymen still use several willows for this purpose.

It is impossible to identify 'siler.' It is a tree or shrub of wet places, and probably some willow.

Flower, spring.

Italian names: Salcio rosso (S. purpurea);
Salcio da pertiche (S. alba).

SARDONIA HERBA.

'Sardoniis . . . amarior herbis' (*Ec.* vii. 41).

Of all the crowfoots none is more acrid than Ranunculus sceleratus, which is held to be the plant here indicated, though, so far from being confined to Sardinia, it is common in wet places throughout Italy, as it is with us. The mere handling of the plant will cause irritation of the skin.

Trees, Shrubs, and Plants of Virgil

The phrase of sardonic laughter seems to be a piece of popular etymology. Homer's word for this laughter is σαρδάνιος, of which the derivation is unknown. The effect of eating our plant is to contort the face, and the resemblance between Homer's adjective and the adjective of Sardinia seems to have made the Romans think that the plant must come from that island, though they could have found it in their own ditches. The small yellow flowers do not attract attention.

Flower, May and June.

SCILLA (*Ge.* iii. 451).

In our passage Virgil speaks of the squill, Urginea scilla, as an ingredient in sheep-wash. It is common on Italian coasts, and its large green bulbs are very conspicuous on the mud-heaps between Crotone and the solitary column which remains of the Temple of Hera on the Lacinian promontory. Our own supplies of the useful drug are said to come chiefly from Spain.

Palladius mentions a curious use for the bulb. It was split in two and the halves tied round the cutting of a fig-tree. It seems to have been an early form of what gardeners call 'bottom heat,' but there cannot have been much of it.

Flower, August to October.
Italian name, Scilla.

Serpyllum

SERPYLLUM.

'olentia late | serpylla' (*Ge.* iv. 30).

The common form of thyme (Thymus serpyllum) is confined to the higher lands in Italy, but the narrow-leaved variety comes somewhat lower down. The plant is Shakespeare's wild thyme, and Milton makes it grow, as it might, on the rocks above a desert cave or grotto. Virgil names it as a bee plant, and the leaves are braised with garlic for the reaper's midday meal.

For garden thyme, which is not a native of England, see Thymum.

Flower, May to September.
Italian name, Pepolino.

SORBUS.

'fermento atque acidis imitantur vitea sorbis' (*Ge.* iii. 380).

There can be no doubt that the passage refers to some kind of beer and some kind of cider, and it has been inferred that both liquors were made in Italy. But Virgil is speaking of Scythians, and a juster inference would be that these liquors were not made in Italy, and that Virgil had heard of them through travellers. At a later date they *were* made in Italy.

The service-tree (Pyrus sorbus) is much like the rowan or mountain ash, but the berries are larger. The fruit is too austere to be eaten until it has been bletted like a medlar, and become brown and soft. It would seem that the Romans had not discovered

121

Trees, Shrubs, and Plants of Virgil

this art, and Martial therefore says that sorbs are fit food only for a slave. There were several varieties of the fruit.

This tree is not native in England, though one tree grows, apparently wild, in Wyre Forest. It must be distinguished from our own wild service-tree, which has smaller berries and undivided leaves. Both are wild in Italy, and the former is cultivated there for its fruit.

> Flower, May and June.
> Italian name, Sorbo.

SUBER.

'silvestri subere' (*Ae.* **xi.** 554).
'corticibus . . . suta cavatis . . . alvearia' (*Ge.* iv. 33).
'tegmina queis capitum raptus de subere cortex' (*Ae.* vii. 742).

The cork-tree (Quercus suber) is a native of central and southern Italy, and the men with cork helmets are Campanians. Though the word 'cortex' is not limited to the bark of the cork-tree, we have Columella's word that this was the best material for hives, and doubtless this was what Virgil meant. When he says that bees sometimes establish themselves 'cavis corticibus,' he uses the word in a wider sense. The farmers who, on the feast of Bacchus, put on masks made of hollow 'cortices,' doubtless used cork when they could get it. Cork was also used as stoppers for wine-jars, tar being smeared over it. Roman ladies, like Trollope's Lady Rosina de Courcey, had cork soles to their winter shoes.

The tree is evergreen, with slightly toothed leaves,

and is of much less stature than the oak. The cup of the acorn is covered with velvety scales.

> Flower, April and May.
> Italian name, Sughera.

TAEDA.

> 'taedas silva alta ministrat' (*Ge.* ii. 431).

Originally the name of a tree, our word more often signifies a torch, and probably has that meaning in this passage. Virgil, however, must have known the material of the tree even if he never saw it alive. It is the Swiss stone-pine (Pinus cembra), a native of lofty mountains, and found on the Alps within sight of the plain of Lombardy. The strong aroma, at its highest point in the spring, points to the very rosinous character which made it of service for torches. The tree has a close, erect, and somewhat oval habit of growth. When Horace compared Hannibal's descent upon Italy to a fire sweeping 'per taedas,' he doubtless was speaking of conifers generally, and had no special kind in view.

> Flower, July.
> Italian name, Pino Zimbro.

TAXUS.

> ' (amant) aquilonem et frigora taxi ' (*Ge.* ii. 113).
> ' taxi torquentur in arcus ' (*ib.* 448).
> ' sic tibi Cyrnaeas fugiant examina taxos ' (*Ec.* ix. 30).

In Italy the yew (Taxus baccata) is exclusively a tree of the higher ground, and except in Liguria does not come near the coast. Virgil says that it is characteristic of cold soils, but with us it is most plentiful on chalky soils (*Ge.* ii. 257). Perhaps Virgil, seeing it flourish with a north aspect, made the false inference that it liked the soil also to be cold. Theophrastus observed that it was a mountain tree and liked shade, but is silent as to the soil.

Our second passage shows that, as in medieval England, the wood of the yew was shaped into bows. The tree was also grown in gardens, and sometimes became the victim of the topiary, though it was the box that more often suffered the indignity of being clipped into animal and inanimate shapes.

Virgil forbids the planting of yews near a bee-hive (*Ge.* iv. 47), and was perhaps right in holding that the flower of the yew made honey bitter. Knowing that Corsican honey had an ill flavour, he seems in our third passage to have assumed that the bitterness was due to this tree. Travellers in Corsica, however, set it down to the box. Arcangeli says that yew is rare in all the islands.

In the passage referred to above concerning soil Virgil calls yews 'nocentes.' The word covers several kinds of damage. Grass will hardly grow under a yew, and the roots extend a long way. The ancients held that both the berries and the leaves were poisonous. I have often eaten the mucilaginous berry, and if there is poison in it it must be in the seeds. Cattle can eat the shoots off the tree ap-

Taxus

parently with impunity, but if they feed on branches that have been gathered and left to ferment they die of it.

> Flower, January to April.
> Italian name, Tasso.

TEREBINTHUS.

' per artem | inclusum buxo aut Oricia terebintho | lucet ebur '
(*Ae.* x. 135).

The terebinth, or turpentine-tree (Pistacia Terebinthus), now grows wild in Italy, and the point of Virgil's epithet is uncertain. According to Servius, a variety with very black wood came from Oricus in Epirus, but it looks as though Servius, after the manner of scholiasts, had concocted his note out of the passage. Virgil did not scruple to couple a foreign name with an Italian tree or plant if the foreign town or country was famous for it. Thus, in spite of all the olives of southern Italy, he calls the fruit ' Sicyonian bacam,' because the Achaean town of Sicyon was famous for its olives.

In Greece, Theophrastus tells us, the wood was not used, and in Italy the art of inlaying, to which our passage refers, was doubtless later than his time, however fashionable it may have become in the later days of the Republic. The Greeks by incision got a rosin from the exudation of the tree. This is now called Chian turpentine, as most of it comes from the Isle of Skio.

> Flower, April and May.
> Italian name, Terebinto.

Trees, Shrubs, and Plants of Virgil

THYMBRA.

'graviter spirantis copia thymbrae' (*Ge.* iv. 31).

The species of savory here named is probably Satureia hortensis, a small labiate annual cultivated for the aromatic tops, which were used in cookery and for flavouring vinegar.   In England this is known as summer savory.   Our plant may, however, be another species, S. montana, known here as winter savory.   It is a shrubby perennial.   Whichever of the two was called thymbra, the other was called satureia, from which name savory is derived.   The Greek θύμβρα was perhaps a third species not native to Italy.

Flower, Summer.

Italian names, Santoreggia and Savoreggia.

THYMUM.

'Cecropium . . . thymum' (*Ge.* iv. 270).
'thymo mihi dulcior Hyblae' (*Ec.* vii. 37).
'redolent . . . thymo fragmantia mella' (*Ge.* iv. 169).

I believe that two species are included under this name, and that the Athenian and the Italian thyme were not the same plant.   The former is admittedly Thymus capitatus, which is found in southern but not in northern Italy.   On the other hand, the species which occurs all along the western side of the peninsula, T. vulgaris, seems not to be found in Greece.   This is the plant still called 'timo' in Italy, and commonly cultivated in our gardens under the name of garden thyme.

Thymum

Thyme was evidently the chief bee plant, though its season of flowering hardly exceeds a month. It was also used for fumigating the hive (*Ge.* iv. 241), and as a medicine for its inhabitants (*ib.* 267). The leaves were also used in cookery, and when it was to be dried for this purpose it was held best to dry it in the shade. Modern authorities agree with this view.

Writers on Shakespeare's wild thyme frequently quote Virgil, but the two poets have different plants in mind.

'Flower, June.
Italian name, Timo.

TILIA.

'(apes) pascuntur . . . pinguem tiliam' (*Ge.* iv. 183).
'tiliae leves' (*Ge.* ii. 449).

The small-leaved lime (Tilia parvifolia) is native in Rockingham Forest and perhaps in a few other places in southern England. In Italy it is confined to the high ground. The limes which the old Corycian grew at Taranto may have been one of the sub-species, either T. intermedia, the common lime, or T. platyphylla, the broad-leaved lime. Virgil gives the Corycian credit for being successful with a hill-land tree at so low an altitude. I take 'pinguem' to refer to the sticky leaves, as in Juvenal's 'pinguia crura luto' and Martial's 'pinguis virga,' a stick plastered with bird-lime. All varieties of the trees seem to be beloved by bees.

The timber, which Virgil commends for the yoke of the plough, is light, and can be planed smooth;

hence it figures both as 'lĕvis' (*Ge.* i. 173), and as 'lēvis' (*Ge.* ii. 449). It is well fitted for carving, and was much used by Grinling Gibbons.

Bass made of the inner bark, 'philyra,' was used for tying flowers into chaplets and garlands.

Flower, June and July.

Italian name, Tiglio.

TRIBULUS: see Lappa.

TINUS.

Philargyrius tells us that in the phrase which appears in our manuscripts as 'tiliae atque uberrima pinus' (*Ge.* iv. 141) Virgil left a choice of two readings, 'pinus' and 'tinus.' The latter is our garden laurustinus (Viburnum tinus), characteristically called ·by Conington 'a kind of wild bay-tree,' though the bay is wild in Italy, and the laurustinus is nowise akin to it. The Corycian grew it for its beauty only, for at Taranto the flowers would be over before his bees were much about.

In *Ge.* iv. 112, 'ipse thymum pinosque ferens de montibus altis,' the Palatine manuscript gives 'tinos' for 'pinos.' This is certainly a false reading. The laurustinus is eminently a tree of the coastland, and flowers in the dead time of the year. Even in Mid-Sussex it suffers some damage in a hard frost, and it would never be so foolish as of its own accord to face a winter in the Apennines.

Flower, January and February.

Italian name, Lauro-tino.

Triticum

TRITICUM.

'triticeam messem' (*Ge.* i. 219).

Wheat (Triticum vulgare), the reputed invention of Osiris, was perhaps developed out of spelt or some other grass in the valley of the Nile. The Italian variety was bearded, as it appears in the statues of Ceres. Though Varro gives us the names for the different parts of the ear, some of the lexicons are not exact. The ear itself is 'spica,' whence 'spicea messis' (*Ge.* i. 314), though Virgil usually avails himself of synecdoche and uses 'arista' in its stead (*Ge.* i. 8, etc.). This is properly the beard, and in 'molli arista' (*Ec.* iv. 28) seems to have that meaning, the epithet applying to the flexibility of the beard. It must, however, be said that 'mollis,' as applied to plants, seems to be a difficult and shifty adjective. The bract, which forms an envelope to the organs of reproduction, is 'gluma,' and the seed or grain of corn is 'granum.' The names of other parts of the plant apply to other cereal grasses as well. Thus 'stipula' and 'culmus' are synonyms for the stem, halm, or straw, while 'palea' is the chaff.

Wheat broke into varieties, the best for colour and weight being 'robus.'

Italian name, Grano.

Trees, Shrubs, and Plants of Virgil

TUS.

'India mittit ebur, molles sua tura Sabaei' (*Ge.* i. 57).
'solis est turea virga Sabaeis' (*Ge.* ii. 117).
'turiferis Panchaïa pinguis harenis' (*ib.* 139).
Cf. *Ae.* i. 417 ; iv. 453 ; xi. 481.

Although Virgil is mistaken in supposing that Arabia or the land of Sheba alone produced frankincense, it is probable that no other country exported it to Rome. Theophrastus tells us that it came from Arabia, and gives travellers' accounts of the tree and the methods of collecting the gum. The Arabians seem to have lost the art of cultivating the tree, for nowadays their product is inferior to that which comes from the islands of the Indian Archipelago.

The tree which produces it is either Boswellia serrata or B. Carteri, perhaps varieties of the same species, which have a balsamic and resinous juice. Its use in religious ceremonies arises from the belief that the smoke carries the scent upward to the noses of the gods.

ULMUS.

'ulmis adiungere vites' (*Ge.* i. 2).
'ulmus opaca ingens' (*Ae.* vi. 283).
'nec gemere aeria cessabit turtur ab ulmo' (*Ec.* i. 59).
'genus haud unum . . . fortibus ulmis' (*Ge.* ii. 83).

Recent investigation has considerably modified our views of the species of elms. The common English elm used to be accounted a Roman importation, but it is now ascertained that the English

Ulmus

and the Roman elms are specifically distinct. Our own retains the name of Ulmus campestris, and appears to be a native of southern England. Its habit of not producing fertile seeds must be ascribed to its power of multiplying itself by suckers rather than by a foreign origin. The Italian species has been named U. australis, and is distinguished by its thicker leaves and their larger and more cuspidate apex. When Virgil tells us that there are several kinds he doubtless means the varieties into which the species easily breaks, and also the wych elm, U. montana, which is found in the higher ground of northern Italy.

The elm was largely planted to support the vines in a vinetum, but seems to have produced nothing that was of use in a vinea. Its timber made the beam of the plough (*Ge.* i. 170), and its leaves served for litter and fodder (*Ge.* ii. 446).

Since elm timber does not readily warp, it was the proper material for ' cardines.' These, with the good leave of the lexicons, are not hinges, but upright beams let into sockets, and having the planks of the door attached to them.

Flower, February and March.
Italian name, Olmo.

Trees, Shrubs, and Plants of Virgil

ULVA.

'ulvam . . . palustrem' (*Ge*. iii. 175).
'viridi procumbit in ulva' (*Ec*. viii. 88).
'in ulva | delitui' (*Ae*. ii. 135).
'informi limo glaucaque . . . in ulva' (*ib*. vi. 416).

This, which one might expect to be among the easiest, is among the more difficult to identify. That the name indicates a species, and is not, as some have supposed, a general name for marsh plants with sword-like leaves, is sufficiently proved by two lists in Ovid's *Metamorphoses*—

'Non illic canna palustris,
nec steriles ulvae, nec acuta cuspide iunci' (iv. 288)—

a passage which describes a limpid Lycian lake; and this description of the scene of a boar-hunt:

'Tenet ima lacunae
lenta salix ulvaeque leves iuncique palustres
viminaque et longa parvae sub harundine cannae' (viii. 335).

It is clear that 'harundo' is Ovid's name for the great or pole reed, Arundo donax, and 'canna' his name for the common reed, Phragmites communis. Our passage and many others show that 'ulva' was a common marsh plant with green leaves, that it grew in masses, and that it was high enough, at least, for a crouching man to hide n. Virgil's epithet of 'glauca' does not help us, because the plant of this passage belongs to the under-world, where are no bright colours and no things of earthly beauty. The reed of Cocytus is 'deformis'

132

(*Ge*. iv. 478), gaunt and ugly, epithets not to be applied to those which fringe the banks of the hallowed Mincio.

Martyn found our plant in the cat's-tail, which children call bulrush, and books by the bookish name of reed-mace; but Ovid would hardly have applied the epithet of 'sterilis' to a plant with so stately an inflorescence. Moreover, the plant has farinaceous and esculent roots, and Martyn himself claims an Italian use for its fluff as the stuffing of beds.

The method of residues seems to leave us with only one plant which answers all the conditions. This is the fen sedge (Cladium Mariscus), whose Italian name is 'paniscastrella di palude.' Its leaves are as long as four and its stem as five feet. It often makes masses in the lakes and marshes of Italy. Though a local plant in England, it is still abundant in some parts of the Eastern Counties fens, and, according to Mrs. Lancaster, was at one time used at Cambridge for lighting fires. It may be recognized by the stout and round stems, which are very leafy, and by the leaves, which have jagged edges and very long points. The flowering cymes are pale brown.

Flower, May and June.
Italian name, Panicastrella di palude.

VACCINIUM: see HYACINTHUS.

Trees, Shrubs, and Plants of Virgil

Verbena.

'verbena tempora vincti' (*Ae.* xii. 120).
'verbenas adole pingues' (*Ec.* viii. 65).
'lilia verbenasque' (*Ge.* iv. 131).

The vervain (Verbena officinalis) is a fairly frequent roadside plant in England and very common in Italy. It has a small spike of bluish flowers, and, as Pliny noted, an angular stem and oak-like leaves. It has not enough beauty or dignity to justify its standing side by side with the lily in the Corycian's garden, nor does it look like a bee plant, and I have never seen bees on it, though I have grown it in a garden. The Corycian must have learnt from his Italian neighbours how highly they valued a plant which could cure them of divers diseases, save them from the effect of a serpent's fang, and through incantation bring an errant husband to his wife's breast. It could cleanse a house from impurities, and Jupiter would have no other herb to sweep his table.

When the Romans held that a foreign State had done them a wrong, they sent an ambassador, who wore a fillet of white wool with a wreath of vervain, plucked root and all on the Capitol, to demand reparation. In this use the plucked tufts were called 'sagmina,' or sacred things, and the envoy was 'verbenarius.' It would seem, however, that other plants could be used if they were plucked from the sacred enclosure. Tufts of grass would do, and, in some cases, sprays of myrtle seem to have been chosen. This led to an extension of the name, 'verbena' standing for any spray—bay, olive, or

Verbena

other—that was used in sacred rites. It may have such a meaning in our first passage.

It does not appear what quality in the vervain won for it this remarkable reverence. The Druids are said to have valued it as highly as the Romans did, and in medieval times it had an equal renown as a charm against witchcraft and a remedy for most ailments. In fact, its only property seems to be a slight astringency.

> Flower, June to September.
> Italian names, Verbena and Vervena.

VIBURNUM.
> 'lenta . . . inter viburna cupressi' (*Ec.* i. 26).

The plant here is assumed to be the wayfaring tree (Viburnum Lantana), apparently on the ground that its Italian name is still 'vavorna.' It is true that the branches of this shrub are flexible, but they hardly look it; in fact, as it grows in the hedges of an English limestone district, it is almost aggressively upright. A kindred species is the wild guelder rose (V. Opulus), which affects damper places. In flower and berry it is much the finer shrub, and from it has sprung the guelder rose, in which the blossoms are barren and the cyme has become globular. Both species are common in Italy. I have an Opulus growing under a tall pine, and like to think that they are as near Virgil's picture as English conditions will allow.

> Flower, April to June.
> Italian names, Vavorna and Lantana.

Trees, Shrubs, and Plants of Virgil

VICIA.

'tenues foetus viciae' (*Ge.* i. 75 ; cf. *ib.* 227).

The vetch or tare (Vicia sativa) is a leguminous plant developed in cultivation from V. angustifolia, a plant common in most parts of Europe and northern Africa. It is an annual, and in the wild form the seeds are very small, hence tenues, though they grow larger in the cultivated type. The plant is grown for fodder, and the Romans were aware that its roots enriched the ground. The reason of this is explained under FABA. After the crop had been mown, the ground was immediately ploughed, and the nitrogen became available for the succeeding crop.

Flower, May and June.

Italian name, Veccia.

VIOLA.

'et nigrae violae sunt et vaccinia nigra' (*Ec.* x. 39).

'molli viola' (*ib.* v. 38 ; *Ae.* x. 39).

'pallentes violas' (*Ec.* ii. 47).

'violaria' (*Ge.* iv. 32).

It seems that the name covers several distinct plants, as did the Greek ἴον. Our first passage, which follows the line of Theocritus,

καὶ τὸ ἴον μέλαν ἐντὶ καὶ ἁ γραπτὰ ὑάκινθος,

refers to the sweet violet (Viola odorata), of which the purple form was known as Sarran—that is, Tyrian. The white form is also found in Italy; but perhaps in our third passage Virgil is translating

Viola

λευκοΐον, which is evidently not a violet, but what gardeners call a soft-wooded plant. It is usual to identify it with the hoary stock (Matthiola incana), still known in Italy as 'violacciocco bianco,' the epithet presumably referring to the hoariness of the leaves and stem. The plant once grew on the Hastings cliffs, and may still occasionally be found at Freshwater Bay in the Isle of Wight. It is the ancestor of our garden Queen and Brompton stocks, and, like the violet, was a garland flower.

The violet was extensively grown not only for bees, but for its scent, and for a purple dye of no great value. Pesto was as famous for violets as for roses.

Flower of Violets, March and April.

Flower of Stock, March to May.

Italian names : Viola (violet).

Fiorbono, Fiorbianco, and Violacciocco bianco (stock).

VISCUM.

'Solet silvis brumali frigore viscum
fronde virere nova, quod non sua seminat arbos,
et croceo foetu teretes circumdare ramos' (*Ae.* vi. 205 sqq.).

Virgil well indicates the curious green-yellow colour of the mistletoe (Viscum album), and its conspicuousness on a leafless tree in winter. The berries were made into bird-lime, and for this purpose were gathered before they were ripe. There are two varieties, and that which has an oval and yellowish

137

berry was held to give a better product than the more common type, of which the berries are round and white.

The trees on which the mistletoe is most commonly parasitic in Italy are apples, pears, poplars, plums, and almonds.

It is supposed that its association with Christmas came from a dedication to Saturn, which made it figure at the Saturnalia.

Flower, March and April.
Italian name, Vischio.

VITIS AND LABRUSCA.

The former is the cultivated and the latter the wild form of the vine (Vitis vinifera), a native of northern Persia, cultivated from prehistoric times. The vine came to Greece, perhaps, by way of Damascus, where it flourishes greatly, and where lately our soldiers have eaten what one of them called 'huge grapes, by bucketfuls.' As chance seedlings, produced by the pilfering of birds, are apt to return to the wild stock, the 'labrusca' has naturalized itself in woods, and occasionally on sea-beaches, in Italy. Homer pictures it as creeping round the entrance of Calypso's island cave, and Virgil in a like position on a Sicilian grotto, 'Antrum | silvestris raris sparsit labrusca racemis' (*Ec.* v. 6). The scanty bunches provided a small grape, of which peasants made a rough and thin wine.

The cultivation of the vine, in its native country

Vitis and Labrusca

and in Syria and Egypt, produced in early days many varieties. In Virgil's days they were yet more numerous, and, after speaking of fifteen, he cuts short his list with the remark that it were as easy to count the Libyan sands or the waves of the Ionian sea (*Ge.* ii. 90-108). We cannot with any certainty identify these varieties or, indeed, be sure that any of them still exist. Grapes change their character with a change of soil, and varieties produced in cultivation, the 'vernae' of the vegetable world, whether vines or apples or other, seldom have in them the sempiternity of the wilding race. The greybeards of to-day sigh in vain for the Ribston pippin. It irks the good tree to be ever in the service of a devouring master; wherefore, after some generations, it fades and languishes, and grows dim and dies.

Nowadays the vine is usually propagated by eyes, but seeds, cuttings, or layers made the choice of ancient Italy; and Virgil decides for the layer, 'propago' (*Ge.* ii. 63), a method still in occasional use. In the vineyard the young plants were set in rows, 'antes' (*ib.* 417), and usually on the principle of the quincunx, which gives the largest allowance of light and air (*ib.* 278). In the young state, the vines are lightly pinched, as gardeners call it, in summer (*ib.* 365, 366), and, when they have filled their allotted space, they are annually pruned back to the old wood (*ib.* 367 sqq.), with intermediate prunings to remove superfluous growths and let in air and sunshine.

Trees, Shrubs, and Plants of Virgil

Of the vineyard there were two types. For one type the technical name seems to have been 'vinea,' though usage is not quite consistent. In this the vines either crept along the ground or were held up by short sticks—Shakespeare's 'pole-clipt vinyard.' Both methods survive in Italy, the sticks nowadays being often a tripod of bamboo canes. This system reduces labour, but the vines are more liable to damage from hailstorms. It does not appear that Virgil mentions it, his use of the name 'vinea' being merely for metrical convenience, and his principles would involve a preference for the 'vinetum' or 'arbustum,' as it was sometimes called. In this the vines were trained to trees, usually elms (*Ec.* ii. 70; *Ge.* i. 2; *ib.* ii. 221). The only other tree mentioned by Virgil is a willow (*Ec.* x. 40), but many others were occasionally used. The plane was rejected rather for its shaling bark than for its large leaves, for in well-managed vineyards no more leaves were allowed on the supporting tree than served to keep it alive (*Ge.* ii. 400; *Ec.* ii. 70). Indeed, when the soil was thin only a single shoot was allowed to grow from the top of the trunk. On the other hand, in rich soil it was usual to have a system of trained branches.

On this method the young vines were at first trained to reeds, or poles, or folded sticks (*ib.* 358 sq.), which reached up to the lowest tier of branches, the name for the tiers being 'tabulata,' or stories. The interval between the tiers was not less than three feet, and no branch was immediately under one in the tier above it. Otherwise, the whipping of the branch and the vine-shoots in the wind would damage the hanging blossoms or fruit.

To keep out beasts, especially the mischievous goat, it was necessary to enclose the vineyard with a hedge (*ib.* 371) of 'paliurus,' or some other thorny shrub, and the soil had to be kept open by deep and frequent hoeing (*ib.* 399 sq.). In fact, as Virgil says, to the work there is no end.

The wide cultivation and the great value of the vine gave rise to a technical vocabulary for its various parts. As with other trees, the name for the main stem was 'truncus.' The rods left on the tree after pruning were 'palmites,' and the eyes or buds on them 'gemmae,' or sometimes 'oculi.' Thus Virgil's sign of spring is accurately expressed, 'laeto turgent in palmite gemmae' (*Ec.* vii. 48). The shoots which spring from the eyes were 'pampini.' These are longest in autumn before the general pruning, hence 'pampineo autumno' (*Ge.* ii. 5). The summer pruning, in which superfluous 'pampini' were removed, was 'pampinatio,' and 'putatio' is also found in this sense, especially in poetry, though it is more properly applied either to the general removal of the 'pampini' in winter, or to the pruning of the supporting elm or other tree. Lexicons have a way of rendering both 'palmes' and 'pampinus' by 'tendril.' This is absurd, for tendrils do not produce buds, nor are they, as tendrils, pruned off, but only as growing on a 'pampinus.' Technically, 'racemus' is the stalk of the bunch of grapes, 'uva,' but is often used for the bunch itself, and once, oddly, by Virgil, for a berry (*Ge.* ii. 60). The berry was 'acinus' or 'acinum,' forms which between them display all three genders. A stone of the grape was 'vinaceum.'

The centurion's staff and whipping-stick, 'nodosa vitis,' was a 'palmes.' Bacchus, for the reins of his team of panthers or tigers, used the young shoots.

Flower, Spring.
Italian name, Vite.

ITALIAN NAMES

WITH THEIR EQUIVALENTS IN VIRGIL

ABETE rosso, Abies.
Acanto, Acanthus.
Acero, Acer.
Aglio, Alium.
Alberello, Populus.
Albatro, Arbutus.
Alloro, Laurus.
Altea, Hibiscum.
Amarecciole, Genista [Broom].
Amello, Amellus.
[Aneto, Anethum ?]
Antiveleno, Inula.
Appeggi, Cedrus.
Appiastro, Melisphyllum.
Arcidiavolo, Lotus [Celtis].
Attacca-mani, Lappa.
Astone, Carduus.
Astro, Amellus.
Avornello, Ornus.

Baccara, Baccar.
Baccellina, Genista [Dyer's Greenweed].
Benefisci, Hibiscum.
Berbena, Verbena.
Bietola, Beta.
Biondello, Lutum.

Bosso or Bossolo, Buxus.
Braglia, Genista [Dyer's Greenweed].
Brula, Myrica.

Calcatreppola, Tribulus.
Calendula, Calta.
Canajoli, Lupinus.
Canna, Harundo [Great Reed].
Canna di Palude, Harundo [Common Reed].
Capogirlo, Ervum.
Carice, Carex.
Castagno, Castanea.
Cedro (see Malus C.).
Cedronella, Melisphyllum.
Cerinta, Cerintha.
Cetriolino, Cucumis.
Chioppo, Acer.
Cicuta, Cicuta.
Cipolla, Cepa.
Cipresso, Cupressus.
Citraggine, Melisphyllum.
Colore, Ebulus.
Corbezzolo, Arbutus.
Coriandola, Coriandrum.
Corniolo or Crogniolo, Cornus.

Trees, Shrubs, and Plants of Virgil

Cotogno (see Malus B.).
Crescione, Nasturtium.

Dittinella, Casia (Daphne).

Ebbio, Ebulus.
Edera or Ellera, Hedera.
Elabro bianco, Helleborus.
Elenio, Inula.
Elice, Elix.
Endivia, Intubum.
Erbacorsa, Casia (Daphne).
Erba Medica, Medica.
Erba-tortora, Cerintha.
Erbella, Inula.
Eschio, Quercus.

Faggio, Fagus.
Fagiolo dall' occhio, Phaselus.
Farnia, Quercus.
Fava, Faba.
Felce capannaja, Filix.
Finocchio, Anethum [Fennel].
Finocchiaccio, Ferula.
Fiorbono, Viola [Stock].
Fiorrancia, Calta.
Fragola or Fravola, Fragum.
Frassino, Fraxinus.
Frumento, Triticum.

Gattice, Populus.
Gelso, Morus.
Giglio, Lilium.
Giglio rosso [*Lilium bulbiferum*] (see Hyacinthus).
Ginepro, Juniperus.
Ginestra, Ginista [Spanish Broom.]

Ginistrella, Ginista [Dyer's Greenweed].
Gioglio, Lolium.
Giracapo, Narcissus [Pheasant's Eye].
Giunco, Juncus.
Granfarro, Far.
Guaderella, Lutum.

Ippofesto, Tribulus.
Ischio, Ligustrum [Privet].

Lattuga, Lactuca.
Lauro-tino, Tinus.
Lebbio, Ebulus.
Leccio, Ilex.
Lentaggine, Tinus.
Lente or Lenticchia, Lens.
Libo, Taxus.
Ligustro, Ligustrum [Privet].
Lino, Linum.
Loglio, Lolium.
Loppo, Acer.
Lotu, Lotus [Celtis australis].
Lupino, Lupinus.

Maggiorana, Amaracus.
Malva, Malva.
Malvaccioni, Hibiscum.
Marruca, Paliurus.
Melo, Malus [Apple].
Miglio, Milium.
Mirto, Myrtus.
Mochi, Ervum.
Moro, Morus.
Mullaghera, Lotus [*L. corniculatus*.
Muschio, Muscus.

Italian Names

Narcisso, Narcissus [Pheasant's Eye].
Nasso, Taxus.
Nocca, Carex.
Nocciuolo, Corylus.
Noce, Nux.

Oleastro, Oleaster.
Olivella, Ligustrum [Privet].
Olivo or Ulivo, Olea or Oliva.
Olmo, Ulmus [*Ulmus australis*].
Olmo riccio, Ulmus [*U. montana*].
Ontano, Alnus.
Orniello, Ornus.
Orzo, Hordeum.

Pallone [*Viburnum Opulus*] (See Viburnum).
Palma da datteri, Palma.
Panicastrella di palude, Ulva.
Pan-porcino or Pan-terreno, Baccar.
Papavero, Papaver.
Pepolino, Serpyllum.
Pero, Pirus.
Persia, Amaracus.
Pino di Corsica, Pieea.
Pino da pinocchi, Pinus [Stone Pine].
Pino di Scozia, Pinus [Scotch Fir].
Pino Zimbro, Taeda.
Platano, Platanus.
Porro, Porrum.
Prungo, Prunus [*Prunus domestica*].
Prugnolo, Prunus [*P. spinosa*].
Pungi-topo, Ruscus,

Ramerino or Rosmarino, Rosmarinus.
Rogo or Rovo, Rubus.
Rombice or Romice, Rumex.
Rosa, Rosa.
Rucola or Ruchetta, Eruca.
Ruta, Ruta.

Sala [*Typha latifolia*. See under Ulva].
Salce, Salix.
Santoreggia or Savoreggia, Thymbra.
Scacciabile, Baccar.
Scarlattina, Cerintha.
Scilla, Scilla.
Sgancio, Prunus [*P. spinosa*].
Sedano, Apium.
Sorbo, Sorbus.
Spaccasassi, Lotus [Celtis].
Spadarella [*Gladiolus zegetum*. See Hyacinth.]
Spelta, Far.
Speronella, Lappa.
Spinogiallo [*Centaurea solstitialis*. See Cardus].
Stroppioni, Carduus [*C. arvensis*].
Sughera, Suber.
Susino, Plum [*Prunus domestica*].

Tamarice, Myrica.
Tasso, Taxus.
Testucchio, Acer.
Tiglio, Tilia.
Timo, Thymum.

Vavorna, Viburnum [*V. Lantana*].

145

Trees, Shrubs, and Plants of Virgil

Veccia, Vicia.
Veladro, Helleborus.
Vena, Avena.
Verbena, Verbena.
Viola, Viola [Sweet Violet].
Violaccio bianco, Viola [Stock].
Vischio (Viscum).

Visciolo, Cerasus.
Vite, Vitis.

Zafferano, Crocus.
Zampino, Abies.
Zinepro, Juniperus.
Zirlo, Ervum.
Zucca, Cucurbita.

This list is compiled from Arcangeli, with a good many additions. The word *scacciabile* seems not to be in the dictionaries, nor have I ever seen it written. I have been told that *Medicago arborea* is called *cytiso*, but Arcangeli does not give it, and it seems to be used of an exotic. For *Saliunca* I have not heard or found any name.

LIST OF SCIENTIFIC NAMES

WITH THEIR EQUIVALENTS IN VIRGIL

Abies pectinata, Abies.
Acacia Arabica, Lotus.
Acanthus mollis, Acanthus.
Acer campestre, Acer.
Aconitum anthora, Aconitum.
Allium cepa, Cepa.
—— porrum, Porrum.
—— sativum, Alium.
Alnus glutinosa, Alnus.
Alhaea officinalis, Hibiscum.
Amomum cardamomum, Amomum.
Anethum graveolens, Anethum (?)
Apium graveolens, Apium.
Arbutus unedo, Arbutus.
Arundo donax, Harundo.
Avena fatua, Avena sterilis.
Avena sativa, Avena.

Beta ciela, Beta.
—— maritima, Beta.
Boswellia, Tus.
Buxus sempervirens, Buxus.

Calendula officinalis, Calta.
Carduus arvensis, Carduus.

Castanea sativa, Castanea.
Celtis australis, Lotus.
Centaurea calcitrapa, Tribulus.
—————— solstitialis, Carduus (?)
Cerinthe aspera, Cerinthe.
Cichorium divaricatum, Intubum.
Citrus medica [see Malus C.].
Cladium mariscus, Ulva.
Conium maculatum, Cicuta.
Coriandrum sativum, Coriandrum.
Cornus mas, Cornus.
Corylus Avellana, Corylus.
Crocus sativus, Crocus.
Cucumis sativus, Cucumis.
Cucurbita pepo, Cucurbita.
Cupressus sempervirens, Cupressus.
Cyclamen (species), Baccar.
Cytisus scoparius, Genista.

Daphne gnidium, Casia.
Dolichus melanophthalmus, Phaselus.

Eruca sativa, Eruca.

147

Trees, Shrubs, and Plants of Virgil

Fagus silvestris, Fagus.
Ferula communis, Ferula.
Foeniculum vulgare, Anethum.
Fragaria vescum, Fragum.
Fraxinus excelsior, Fraxinus.
——— ornus, Ornus.

Galium aparine, Lappa.
Genista tinctoria, Genista.
Gladiolus communis [see Hya-
   cinthus].

Hedera helix, Hedera.
Hedera chrysocarpa, Hedera
   pallens.
Hordeum vulgare, Hordeum.

Inula helenium, Inula.

Juglans regia, Nux.
Juncus conglomeratus and J.
   effusus, Juncus.
Juniperus communis, Juniperus.

Lactuca sativa, Lactuca.
Laurus cinnamomum, Casia.
Laurus nobilis, Laurus.
Lepidium sativum, Nasturtium.
Ligustrum vulgare, Ligustrum.
Lilium bulbiferum [see Hyacin-
   thus].
——— candidum, Lilium.
——— croceum [see Hyacin-
   thus].
——— martagon [see Hyacin-
   thus].
Linum angustifolium and L.
   usitatissimum, Linum.
Lolium temulentum, Lolium.
Lupinus albus, Lupinus.

Malva silvestris, Malva.
Matthiola incana, Viola pallens.
Medicago arborea, Cytisus.
— ——— sativa, Medica.
Melissa officinalis, Melisphyl-
   lum.
Morus nigra, Morus.
Myrtus communis, Myrtus.

Narcissus poeticus, Narcissus.
——— serotinus, Narcissus
   sera comans.

Olea Europaea, Oleaster.
—— sativa, Olea and Oliva.
Origanum dictamnum, Dic-
   tamnum.
——— marjorana, Amaracus.

Paliurus aculeatus [= australis],
   Paliurus.
Panicum miliaceum, Milium.
Papaver hortense, P. officinale,
   and P. somniferum, Papaver.
Phoenix dactylifera, Palma.
Phragmites communis, Har-
   undo.
Pinus cembra, Taeda.
—— laricio, Picea.
—— pinea, Pinus.
—— silvestris, Pinus.
Pistacia terebinthus, Terebin-
   thus.
Platanus orientalis, Platanus.
Populus alba, Populus.
Prunus cerasus, Cerasus.
——— communis, Prunus.
——— domestica, Prunus.
——— insititia, Prunus.

148

List of Scientific Names

Prunus spinosa, Spinus.
Pteris aquilina, Filix.
Pyrus cydonia [see Malus B.].
—— domestica, Pirus.
—— malus, Malus.
—— sorbus, Sorbus.

Quercus ilex, Ilex.
—— pedunculata, Quercus and Robur.
—— sessiliflora, Aesculus and Robur.
—— suber, Suber.

Ranunculus sceleratus, Sardonia herba.
Reseda luteolum, Lutum.
Ros marinus, Rosmarinus officinalis.
Rosa (species), Rosa.
Rubus discolor and others, Rubus.
Rumex crispus and others, Rumex.
Ruscus aculeatus, Ruscus.
Ruta graveolens, Ruta.

Salix (species), Salix.
Sambucus ebulus, Ebulus.
Satureia hortensis, Thymbra.

Satureia thymbra, Thymbra.
Siler, Salix (?)
Spartium junceum, Genista.

Tamarix Gallica, Myrica.
Taxus baccata, Taxus.
Thymus serpyllum, Serpyllum.
—— vulgaris, Thymum.
Tilia parvifolia, Tilia.
Triticum spelta, Far.
—— vulgare, Triticum.

Ulmus australis, Ulmus.
—— montana, Ulmus.
Urginea Scilla, Scilla.

Vaccinium [see Hyacinthus].
Valeriana Celtica, Saliunca.
Veratrum album, Helleborus.
Verbena officinalis, Verbena.
Viburnum Lantana, Viburnum.
—— tinus, Tinus.
Vicia ervilia, Ervum.
—— faba, Faba.
—— lens, Lens.
—— sativa, Vicia.
Viscum album, Viscum.
Vitis vinifera, Vitis and Labrusca.